Illuminated
Spirit

Illuminated Spirit

Conversations with a Kyudo Master

Dan and
Jackie DeProspero

KODANSHA INTERNATIONAL
Tokyo • New York • London

Distributed in the United States by Kodansha America, Inc., 114 Fifth Avenue, New York, N.Y. 10011, and in the United Kingdom and continental Europe by Kodansha Europe Ltd., 95 Aldwych, London WC2B 4JF. Published by Kodansha International Ltd., 17-14 Otowa 1-chome, Bunkyo-ku, Tokyo 112, and Kodansha America, Inc.

First edition, 1996.
96 97 98 99 10 9 8 7 6 5 4 3 2 1

ISBN 4-7700-1970-X

Library of Congress Cataloging-in-Publication Data

DeProspero, Dan.
    Illuminated spirit : conversations with a kyudo master / Dan and Jackie DeProspero.
        p.   cm.
    Includes index.
    ISBN 4-7700-1970-X
    1. Archery–Japan. 2. Archery–Japan–Philosophy. 3. Onuma, Hideharu, 1910-1990. I. DeProspero, Jackie. II. Onuma, Hideharu, 1910-1990. III. Title.
    GV1188. J3D47 1996
    799.3'2'0952–dc20   96-43498
                                                CIP

For
Michael, Mika,
Dylan and Ian

CONTENTS

Acknowledgments

The authors are indebted to a number of people without whose help and encouragement this book would not have been possible. We owe our greatest debt of gratitude, of course, to Onuma-sensei, who treated us not as students but as members of his family. And we owe a special thank-you to Onuma-sensei's wife and daughters, who continue to treat us like family long after his death. Their warmth, generosity and unending support was in large part responsible for the making of this book. By sharing with us their recollections of Onuma-sensei's life, and allowing us access to old family records and photographs, they greatly enhanced the book's quality and immediacy.

We are also grateful to the many friends, former students and colleagues of Onuma-sensei's around the world who shared with us their insight into his life and teachings. We would also like to thank our teachers and fellow students at the Toshima-ku Kyudo Renmei for their kindness and patience in answering our questions as we struggled to learn more about kyudo and about Onuma-sensei.

We are grateful to the staff of Kodansha International,

and especially to Kuramochi Tetsuo, who lent this project his enthusiastic support from its inception. A special thank-you must also go to our editor, Elizabeth Floyd, who spent many long hours reviewing the text. Her guidance and hard work are greatly appreciated.

Finally, we must thank our parents and our brothers and sisters for their patience and support as we pursued our dreams half a world away from home. We hope that in some small way this book will compensate for all the birthdays, holidays and family gatherings we missed during our long stay in Japan.

It should be noted that all Japanese personal names are written in the traditional Japanese style of family name first. Also, for the sake of simplicity, diacritical marks were intentionally omitted from the text. Unless otherwise noted, all photographs and illustrations are the property of either the Onuma family or the authors.

Any factual errors or misinterpretations that may appear in the text are the sole responsibility of the authors.

Introduction

It was early in 1981 that we left the United States for Japan with one-year working visas and contracts to teach English at a language school in Tokyo. That in itself is a story of good fortune, good friends and perfect timing. We had both been interested for many years in the arts and culture of Japan and when the offer came—thanks to the efforts of a dear Japanese friend—to live and work in Japan for a year, we accepted immediately. To our way of thinking, this was like a year's paid holiday in a place we had always dreamed about. Neither of us suspected that our little holiday would extend to more than a third of our lifetimes.

Once we had settled in, we began to immerse ourselves in the culture. Our work schedules were such that we could spend most of every day pursuing other interests: we studied tea ceremony, painting, swordsmanship and aikido, often one after another, until it was time to go to work. At that point we still believed we would be returning home at the end of the year, and were determined to absorb as much of the culture as possible in the time we had left. In that same spirit we decided to accompany a friend to her practice of kyudo (traditional Japanese archery). This was a decision that would change the course of our lives. We had heard about kyudo before, we knew it was the study of traditional Japanese archery, and although we both knew very well that we were too busy to fit its study into our schedule, still we were excited to have an opportunity to observe it firsthand.

As soon as we entered the training hall we saw the sensei (teacher), Master Onuma Hideharu, seated with some students at a low table having tea. He immediately got to his feet and walked over to greet us; then, speaking in English, he welcomed us to the class. We were escorted to the seat of honor directly in front of the practitioners and watched the class with Onuma-sensei at our side. He was very gracious, open and genuine, and took great care to explain the practice and philosophy of kyudo to us. We were so taken with his gentle manner and obvious strength of character that we decided on the spot to rearrange our schedules to allow us to study under this extraordinary man.

The practice of kyudo began to consume an ever greater portion of our free time until it became clear that this was something we were going to do for the rest of our lives. Needless to say we extended our teaching contracts and continued our study of kyudo. In 1985 our relationship with Onuma-sensei deepened when we moved into his apartment above the archery equipment shop he and his family operated. From that point we studied kyudo full-time under his guidance, until his death in 1990. We continued to live with the family until we returned to the United States in 1995.

To this day we do not know just why Onuma-sensei

chose to give his teachings to us. It was an unusual situation to be sure. Not only were we non-Japanese but we possessed only a basic knowledge of the native language, and even less understanding of kyudo itself. Perhaps it was as simple as being in the right place at the right time. We were young and worked part-time schedules that permitted us to spend the better part of each day in his company, while he was getting older and felt ready to pass his teachings on to the next generation. In any case, we were very fortunate and have always felt that the information we were given was never intended for us alone. Sensei was sharing it with us because he trusted us to share it with others. In our first book, *Kyudo: The Essence and Practice of Japanese Archery*, we tried to pass along the bulk of his teachings on the art of kyudo. But it is with this book that we finally feel we have begun to share the true knowledge and wisdom of the extraordinary man whom we called both teacher and friend.

Onuma-sensei was a patient man, always open to our questions. He seemed to live by the axiom that the only stupid question is the one never asked. But more than anything else, he always encouraged us to seek the answers on our own. Knowledge, he said, may originate with the teacher, but learning originates with the student. As a result he rarely gave a complete answer the first time a particular question arose. Sometimes he refused to answer at all. Perhaps most frustrating was his habit of embedding important lessons in simple analogies or seemingly irrelevant conversations on topics as varied as fishing, food or current events. Unfortunately it's almost certain that in the early days of our training we missed a good deal of his teaching simply because we failed to see what he was actually trying to tell us. Confusing as his teaching techniques could be at times, we eventually adjusted and also resigned ourselves to the fact that we were going to have to put a lot more effort into our attempts to understand.

The reader will find that this book is a blend of Onuma-sensei's teachings and the interpretations we made of them on the basis of our study of kyudo. The reader should by no means accept our understanding of the teachings as the only one possible. We would urge readers to carefully read between the lines to extract teachings that may be especially relevant to them.

It is also important to understand that some of these conversations actually represent a compilation of a number of exchanges that took place over a period of several years and that are combined here for the sake of clarity. Still the reader may find some of the information contained in the various chapters repetitive. Actually, repetition was a favorite teaching technique of Onuma-sensei. He was always anxious to connect his teachings to the subject at hand, which caused him to give the same teaching over and over again in different contexts until we finally picked up on the message. Throughout our apprenticeship we always found that this technique eventually led to a fuller, more personal understanding of the essence of his teaching. We employ the technique in this book for the same reason.

It is impossible to fully document the sources of Onuma-sensei's teachings. Most of the teachings are unmistakably his own. But he was a well-read man with over seventy years of experience in the art of kyudo, and some of his thoughts and teachings undoubtedly evolved from those of others. Onuma-sensei always said that his teachings amounted to nothing more than common sense.

He often seemed amused when one of us would get all excited about something that he considered obvious. Naturally, many of his teachings are based on traditional Eastern thought, but the reader will find in them a hint of conventional Western wisdom as well. To us the way they resonate with both East and West suggests a universal quality. And in the modern world, where technology makes it easy for people to destroy one another, wisdom that unites the great philosophical traditions becomes more relevant than ever before.

Onuma-sensei was a great kyudo master but at the same time he was a man like any other. He was neither a god nor a guru, and he would have resisted being depicted as either. Yet his words held a great deal of wisdom. This wisdom had then, and continues to have, a tremendous influence on the lives of all who were lucky enough to come into contact with him. We believe that Sensei's teachings as sketched in the following chapters will draw readers back again and again, allowing them to find some fresh insight or something of rare and personal value that they failed to see on first reading. When that happens, we will have been successful in transferring the power and promise of Onuma-sensei's words to these pages.

Dan and Jackie DeProspero
November 1996

◁ 1 ▷

Inspiration

Kyudo, perhaps more than any other martial art, is considered to be an excellent spiritual discipline when practiced under the tutelage of an inspirational teacher. It would be hard to imagine a teacher more inspirational than Onuma-sensei. He repeatedly told us that if we practiced diligently and made a real effort, kyudo could help us change our lives for the better. We once asked him if the practice of kyudo could also help rid the world of evil, or at least change it for the better. As silly and naive as our question must have sounded, he did take the time to answer that great philosophers have tried, for thousands of years, to address the question of good and evil, and that human beings have been trying to change the world from the first day of their existence—and yet humanity still struggles with the same questions.

Onuma-sensei always stressed that his intention was simply to teach us kyudo, not to teach us how to change the world. He also made it quite clear that neither was he trying to change us, adding that no one has the power to effect real change in others. Many people, deep down, are

Onuma Hideharu, headmaster of the centuries-old *Heki-ryu sekka-ha* school of archery, in meditation

waiting for someone else to take charge of their lives and hand over a prescription for what to do or say in a given situation. For Onuma-sensei, kyudo was a means of observing, understanding and changing his own life. He worked only on himself, believing that each of us is totally and completely responsible for improving his own character. Sensei had faith that if every human being were to approach life this way, the result would be smoother relationships, a more caring society and, ultimately, a better world to live in.

Can it really be so simple? The cynic will say that Onuma-sensei sounds like a man who would have students isolate themselves from other people's problems in order to better themselves. But this is far from what he meant, as can be seen in one of his favorite analogies, of two people climbing a mountain:

The mountain looms equally high before us all. And the goal and the struggle we face is the same. The only difference between us lies in the fact that I started climbing long before you. Now when you look ahead you see me in a place where you too would like to be. If I allow myself to look back then I can see that in comparison with you I have come a long way. But I don't like to look back because that hinders my own progress. Just like you, I'm always looking ahead toward the top of the mountain. But this doesn't mean that I ignore others as I climb. I must always be ready to help those who follow. There is a great difference between looking back to compare yourself with the progress of others and looking back to guide others as they climb.

The point he is making is that one should follow a virtuous path simply because it is a good and proper thing to do, not from any expectation of compensation, glory or praise for our efforts. The reward lies in the act itself. And in the knowledge that having traveled that path we can then act as a guide to the others who will surely follow.

The Pursuit of Goals

Some years ago a fellow student questioned Onuma-sensei's use of the English word "goal" during a teaching session. The student said that the use of this word implied a desire for some form of recognition, and asked if such a desire wouldn't be a negative element that would interfere with one's search for the truth. Obviously he had ignored the fact that Onuma-sensei was not a native speaker of English and had no doubt picked the word for its familiarity; originally a loan-word, "goal" has now made its way into everyday Japanese. In any case, we decided to follow up on this line of thought in a subsequent conversation. Onuma-sensei said that his precise choice of words was irrelevant; that his purpose was simply to encourage us to aspire to the ultimate in human possibility. He never defined those possibilities for us, saying only that we

Onuma-sensei (right) as a younger man, performing *Ogasawara-ryu* ceremonial archery

must strive to attain perfection. In the next breath, however, he hinted that it is not humanly possible to achieve that goal, saying that the reward comes not from the attainment of perfection but from its unending pursuit.

That short exchange had a profound effect on both of us. Until that time we had practically worried ourselves sick trying to advance from one stage of training to the next. We knew that our time in Japan was limited, and were determined to reach the goals we had set for ourselves when we first began. But Onuma-sensei made us see that we were focusing on the end rather than the journey, and that the end did not exist without the journey. From then on our training became richer and more fulfilling. Before too long we began to consider how often we focus on goals in other areas too, and we now make conscious efforts to spend what precious time we have on this earth concentrating on life's journey rather than worrying about the end.

The Essence of Things

Onuma-sensei always stressed that in order to improve at anything we need to practice diligently, but that practice alone was not enough. We must also be inspired and hold onto our ideals, because without them our practice is weak and shallow. To truly understand a thing we must search for its essence. Skill, though important, only leaves us with a taste of the truth of a thing. When we watch someone who is technically skilled but who lacks understanding of the essence of his own actions we get the feeling that something is missing. The actions may be correct and the movements precise, but we are left unmoved by the performance. It is as if all meaning and purpose had been ignored in favor of technical expertise. The performance is devoid of the thing most crucial to its success: essence.

To Onuma-sensei that essence is a product of the human spirit that lies deep within us all. When we tap into the human spirit and bring its power to the fore, it serves as a foundation upon which to build technical skills, adding depth and feeling to the performance. Often the spirit lies dormant, numbed by modern life. But the spirit can be coaxed to the surface in a variety of ways. One method, controlled breathing, is used extensively in a number of disciplines and will be discussed at length below. Another method is controlled movement. Onuma-sensei was unequaled in his ability to move with such grace, dignity and strength of spirit that his entry into a room full of people invariably drew the attention of everyone present. He insisted that before one could learn kyudo one must first learn to do simple standing, sitting and walking exercises. More importantly, he stressed that the discipline and concentration needed to perform these exercises correctly would ultimately reward one with a heightened sense of confidence, stability and self-awareness that would enter into every aspect of one's daily life.

The exercises shown here are derived from the practice of kyudo. They have little or no relevance to the way one moves while actually going about a normal routine, but this is precisely why they work. Since they substantially differ from more usual ways of moving they require a good deal more effort and concentration and are less apt to be performed mechanically. To practice the exercises one should feel that every action is connected to the rhythm of one's breathing, for breath and spirit are one and the same. As you start a motion, breathe in slowly and steadily, controlling the flow of breath without straining. Then, as you finish, exhale in the same way. At all times breath and movement alike should be measured, yet fluid.

Onuma-sensei demonstrates the proper way to stand

Walking

Sitting

24

Start from a kneeling position and, keeping the upper body straight, rise slowly and smoothly. Onuma-sensei taught that the body should rise as smoke rises. Meanwhile, slide the left foot forward, keeping it flat against the floor. As you complete the move, slide the right foot forward until it is even with the left foot. Do not permit the body to rock to either side or to shift up and down as you stand.

When you walk, think of moving not from the feet but from the center of the hips, while letting the legs glide underneath the upper body. Do not stiffen the legs but do not let them bend excessively as you move. At all times the upper body should be held straight and should not be allowed to move from side to side. Move by sliding the feet across the floor in smooth, even steps. To turn to the right, slide the right foot straight ahead, so that the toes extend to about the center of the left foot, then turn both the right foot and the upper body,

at the same time, ninety degrees. Let the right foot slide forward slightly. Then turn the left foot ninety degrees and slide it ahead of the right foot, to continue the walking sequence. Walk in a straight line or, if space permits, walk and turn at right angles until you arrive back at your starting point.

To sit, reverse the footwork of the standing sequence, sinking slowly into position. Slide the right knee along the floor until it is even with the left knee, as you lower the body into the final kneeling position.

Pause for a moment in a seated position, then repeat the entire sequence of standing, walking and sitting. Practice the exercises repeatedly, but stop when you become tired and no longer have good control over your posture or movements.

Never rush the breathing or allow the movement to become sluggish. For longer sequences the process of breathing in and out must be made fluid by bridging the natural pause between breaths with a continued feeling of movement, creating what Onuma-sensei called "the sensation of using your whole body to move your little finger." If you can develop this sense, you will experience a renewed sensitivity to your surroundings that has been missing since early childhood. That feeling is evidence that you have become much more attuned to the power of the human spirit.

Developing the Spirit

We once spoke with a man who argued that it was a waste of time for anyone involved in the study of kyudo to speak of spiritual development. His theory was that the acquisition of technical ability was first and foremost, and that energy should only be turned toward development of the spirit later in life. His reasoning is good and there are many who agree with him. Every teacher has experienced the frustration of trying to teach students whose curiosity about more advanced material hinders their ability to learn the basics. But Onuma-sensei was not insensitive to the problem. He too stressed that technique is "the stairway to the spiritual level." The study of technique, in any field, is an important part of the learning experience. But being overly dependent on technique is self-limiting. His solution was to seek a balance. "There is a time to study technique and a time to forget it," he would say. When you learn something new you must practice it until it gets into your bloodstream and becomes a natural part of you. Then you must let it go.

For Onuma-sensei spiritual development was too important to leave to the later years of training. He likened the growth of the spirit to that of a tree:

If, someday, you want to have a strong, beautiful pine that towers above your home and garden, when do you plant the seed? Do you wait until you are old and feeble? I think not. You must plant the seed early and nurture it carefully over the years. It grows as you do—stronger and grander each day.

One day we both learned a valuable lesson about nurturing the spirit, after one of us had managed to hit nine out of ten arrows shot. This was the first time either of us had done so well and when this result was mentioned to Onuma-sensei he answered that missing one arrow was much worse than missing them all. He explained that if we were having an off day, then we could work on our technique and find a solution to the problem, but missing one shot was a sign not of some technical difficulty but of a gap or point of vulnerability in the flow of the spirit. A gap can open up when we become pleased with our progress or, conversely, worried about successfully continuing. In either case concern with matters irrelevant to the shooting cuts us off from the natural flow of our own spirit.

Onuma-sensei emphasized that to keep the spirit strong and flowing smoothly we must move into a state of consciousness known as *mushin,* a Buddhist concept that translates literally as "no mind." For most of us, the concept seems foreign because we associate "no mind" with "no thought"—unconsciousness or even death. But *mushin* is not the elimination of thought; it is the elimination of the remnants of thought: that which remains when thought is divorced from action. In *mushin,* thought and action

28

The breath is key to achieving a state of *mushin*,
or "no mind"

occur simultaneously. Nothing comes between thought
and action, and nothing is left over. But how do we arrive
at such a state when we are constantly bombarded by extra-
neous thought? One technique is to fill the intervals with
the rhythm of the breath. When unwanted thoughts arise,
sweep them aside by concentrating on your breathing cycle.

You may find it difficult at first to concentrate on your breathing while you go about your normal activities. But you can develop the skill by taking a few moments each day to sit quietly and practice breathing. Onuma-sensei taught us to begin by inhaling and exhaling quietly but fully, and without straining. Count each cycle of inhalation and exhalation as one, silently keeping track of your breathing until you reach the number twenty. Repeat the counting process until you develop an intuitive sense of the timing. After that you can leave off counting. Like anything new the technique will, at first, require a good deal of concentrated effort. Eventually, however, it will become second-nature and you will be able to do it with ease as you go about your daily life. It is then that you will begin to feel the power of your spirit grow stronger with each passing day.

Onuma-sensei's students at the Toshima-ku Kyudojo in Tokyo meditate before practice

Faith and Superstition

Onuma-sensei taught that superstition had no place in the practice of kyudo. He told us that we must distinguish between superstition and faith. He defined superstition as something that has a negative influence on our lives, as when a person comes to depend on some lucky object to the point where he feels he cannot perform at his best without it. Sensei said that that was a sign of a weak spirit. On the contrary, believing in something is very important. But belief must be positive, benefiting not only ourselves but others as well. That is what he called faith.

To Onuma-sensei that faith manifested itself in what he called "service rendered to God." He told us that he believed God had given him the talent and the opportunity to do kyudo and that it was, therefore, his responsibility to study as hard as he could. He told us that when he shot he always tried to make the sequence as noble and elegant as he could because God was watching him. "If I do my best," he said, "God will appreciate my effort and shoot for me."

Even though Onuma-sensei had a distinct set of beliefs about the relationship between God and the practice of kyudo he was adamant that kyudo itself was not a religion. Kyudo is simply another path in the search for truth. In that way it shares a common ground with religion, philosophy, the arts, our work and relationships. Each adds value and purpose to our lives and provides us with love, security, hope and a sense of self-worth. In short, each helps us to meet the challenges of life. Since each choice complements the others we should all be free to choose a path that is right for us without inviting conflict from those who have chosen another way.

Conflict and Harmony

We have often wondered why conflict is so prevalent in today's society. It's sometimes especially surprising when conflict erupts within a group or organization whose charter is based on ideals of peace, harmony and goodwill. It seems that almost every such organization—religions, charitable societies, peace groups, community service associations—is eventually troubled by discord among its membership.

We asked Sensei how people with shared ideals and good intentions can become mired in disagreements and infighting. He answered, as he so often did, with an analogy:

When you want to build a new home you start with an ideal image of that home. To actually start the construction you must consult with others who have specific skills—designers, carpenters and masons—and who, using their own techniques and tools, will build the house according to your wishes. Each may be a professional who knows the job well but if they are permitted to build without following a larger plan the result will be a disaster. However, their knowledge and experience may allow them to see some flaw in the original design that you had missed. Ignoring their suggestions could result in a house that is unfit to live in. The key to success is remembering that everyone is working together to create the perfect home. It is not the style of carpentry, the choice of windows or the type of roof that is most important, but the development of harmony among the people working on the home. When harmony is established, then all will work unselfishly toward a common end: the completion of a home that any one of them would be pleased to live in.

That is a simple analogy, not unlike many others, but it instantly made us realize that all too often pride takes precedence over principle. We also realized that the two of us were personally guilty of self-serving behavior, and that this behavior was an undeniable source of disharmony in our lives at the time. Onuma-sensei never scolded us in so many words, but in this case it was clear that the message was intended for the two of us. Sensei then kindly added that everyone, himself included, sometimes indulges in such behavior. The solution is to realize that harmony can prevail only when each of us takes the time to find and hold onto our common humanity.

◁ 2 ▷

Everyday Life

Think back to when you were young and had your whole life planned out. All you needed to make it complete was a loving family, a few good friends, a great job and good health. Unfortunately, we all eventually discover that life does not always go as planned. Even in the best of cases it's rare that we're not confronted with some kind of complication in our daily life. Difficulty with family and friends, trouble in the workplace and health problems both major and minor are just some of the factors in the stress and tension we all experience regularly. We could try, as so many people do, to anticipate and fend off all potentially troublesome situations, but of course total control is not humanly possible. It is possible, however, to control our reactions to a situation. In kyudo, for example, we learn that a poor attitude inevitably results in poor shooting. Anxiety over the poor results only leads to anger at the situation, and at everything and everyone associated with it. Our reaction does not solve the problem but adds to its severity. Instead of trying to anticipate and head off every potential problem, we would do better to look inside ourselves for the means to control our reactions.

Dealing with Anger

In all the years that we lived and studied with Onuma-sensei we never once saw him lose his temper. He sometimes became forceful in his tone of voice in order to control a tense situation but he never resorted to the use of naked anger the way so many of us do in stressful situations. We once asked if he ever got angry. He answered that he had as a younger man, but now found that anger took so much energy that he preferred to find a way around it.

Onuma-sensei's ideas about dealing with anger in our daily lives became clear to us during a meeting we attended with him in which the discussion among some members of the group had become quite heated. Since Onuma-sensei was the highest-ranking member, each faction tried to gain his sympathy but he would not take sides or even offer comment. The tension built to an almost unbearable point and we thought that perhaps he should step in and put an end to the discussion, but he did not do anything. He just sat there, silently and without expression, letting the participants have their say. Because we were new to Japan we could understand almost nothing of what was being said, so we too sat silently and watched. Suddenly we began to notice that the room was growing quieter. One by one the voices of dissension were becoming fewer, until only two remained. Everyone had had their say and the discussion had boiled back down to the point at which it had apparently begun: a disagreement between those two people. Once the cacophony let up, the pair began to talk more reasonably

We never once saw Onuma-sensei lose his temper

and the problem was eventually solved amicably. Only once during the entire incident did Onuma-sensei speak, and that, we were later told, was to admonish someone for bringing into the argument the name of a person who was not present.

We asked Onuma-sensei why he allowed the tension to build that way. He told us that if we get angry when we are shooting poorly it only makes things worse. Everyone knows this but when we are caught up in a tense situation, irritation can blind us to reason. Anger does not dissipate when you set down the bow in disgust. It only festers inside you, growing stronger until it can be released in another, often totally unrelated, situation. A good teacher, therefore, will guide you through the conflict until it is resolved completely. He explained that although it did not look that way, he was in fact very actively involved with the direction the argument took. Because of his position, anything he said would deflect the argument away from its source. It was better to let it run its course and bring everything out into the open while all concerned were present so that the matter could be settled once and for all. Finally, we asked him how he could cope with all the anger in the room, explaining that while we did not know the source of the argument we, nevertheless, found ourselves growing increasingly upset as we became caught up in it. He laughed and said that anger is like a swarm of mosquitoes looking for a victim in a room full of people. You can sit there and wait for the inevitable bite or you can simply blow them away when you feel them buzzing around. His meaning, we believe, was that the sources of anger are many, as are its potential victims. But each of us can use the power of our "breath," or spirit, to ward off anger, whatever its causes or form may be.

Onuma-sensei's thoughts on managing anger are not especially revolutionary. Psychiatrists have been saying for years that in order to deal with our anger we must first recognize its source. Often, however, the anger we feel in a given situation is born from a totally separate and unrelated event, making it difficult to accurately track it down. But there are generally only two possible sources for the anger we feel: we can either be angry at ourselves for our own failings or mistakes, or we can be angry at others for

The bow fully tensed

what we perceive as their failings or slights against us. The modern trend is to focus blame on external sources: parents, teachers, spouses, the political party currently in power or society as a whole. But Onuma-sensei always taught that it is useless to blame problems on others; that the only source we can and should concern ourselves with is the one within ourselves.

To do that one must first understand the difference between accepting responsibility for what happens and faulting oneself for it. In the practice of kyudo if we execute a poor release we do not curse the glove or arrow because they did not perform correctly. If the bow should unexpectedly break we cannot blame it for doing so. It does not break of its own accord and it is the archer alone who must accept responsibility for its care. This does not necessarily mean that the archer is to blame; it simply means that acting in a responsible manner is the best response. Directing one's emotions toward the bow is not going to alter the situation. On the contrary, it will only make it worse. Likewise, shifting the focus from the immediate source of the problem serves no useful purpose. It allows for temporary avoidance of conflict but increases the likelihood of greater problems later. Onuma-sensei liked to say that the time to put out a fire is not when you see the flames but when you smell the smoke. In the same way, the time to work through conflict is generally when it arises.

Using Stress Positively

But what of situations where stress is present in the absence of anger? For many people, nervous tension can be as debilitating as anger. We, for instance, feel that the heavy stress that accompanies a test or demonstration

Tests are held at Meiji Shrine to determine kyudo rankings

prevents us from doing our best. When we asked Onuma-sensei for help with this he told us that we were having trouble because we were trying to eliminate the stress, and because we were unsuccessful this only created more stress. Stress is often considered a bad thing, but this need not be so. Onuma-sensei always gave the example of the beautiful sound a taut bowstring makes when it is plucked by an expert hand. The sound is quite similar to the clear, beautiful tones produced by a musical instrument. The key to using tension positively is to first identify its source, then use that knowledge to keep the tension from becoming disruptive and, ultimately, destructive.

At a test or demonstration, for example, tension fills the air, but this can be put to positive use. Everyone present wants to see you do your best. They do not come hoping to see a poor demonstration, or to see you fail an examination. Even if there are one or two people there with such motives they are in the minority and their negativity is easily overwhelmed by the positive atmosphere created by the rest. Your own doubt and fear create negative tension but you must not allow that to overpower you. Instead of dwelling on your own thoughts of failure or embarrassment, think of all the positive energy radiating from the crowd who are there to see you do your best.

In your workplace, your supervisors do not wish for you to fail in your responsibilities. Their job is made easier if you succeed. If they become upset, try not to be upset by what they say. Think only that they are giving you a clear message of what they expect from you. That makes your job easier. You should be thankful that you now have a clear idea of what is expected of you, since this will help you prevent the same thing from happening again. For the supervisors' part, they should make their needs known clearly from the start so that problems will not arise later.

Onuma-sensei also said that another problem we had when dealing with stress and tension in kyudo was that we were ignorant of the importance of that very stress and tension. The image of kyudo is one of peace and tranquility. People tend to overlook the tremendous effort involved in shooting. When we draw the bow we place it, the string and many of our muscles under considerable stress—without that stress there can be no shot. A certain amount of mental tension is necessary too. We call that concentration. To shoot well we must learn to harness stress and tension so that they become positive elements in our practice.

It is important to remember that stress and tension, in various forms, are integral parts of our daily life: night and day, woman and man, heat and cold, and strength and softness are all combinations of natural opposites held together in harmonious balance precisely because of the tension between them. By refusing to acknowledge the tension that binds life's contrasting elements we downplay much of the excitement and vitality that makes life worth living.

Ordinary Mind

Advanced practitioners of kyudo work to create a state of mental and physical calm that gradually becomes a normal part of their everyday life; this state is known as *heijoshin* ("ordinary mind"). An ordinary mind is one that is calm, well-balanced and disciplined at all times—even when confronted with unexpected events or unpleasant circumstances. This allows us to function more efficiently as we go about our daily routine, yet remain unperturbed by unexpected turns of events. According to Onuma-sensei the secret to achieving an ordinary mind is to treat ordinary moments as special; then special events will seem everyday.

Do you ever pay attention to the trees and flowers around you; do you notice the color of the sky or feel the softness of the breeze? Are you so hemmed in by the commitments of your daily life that you go through the day without noticing any of this? These things are simple and ordinary, but if you miss them you are missing the better part of life. There is a simple remedy. Use the senses that you

*were born with to observe and appreciate all that sur-
rounds you. The person who has come close to dying
learns to revel in the beauty and uniqueness of each
moment, understanding that this is exactly what life is all
about. You can wait until it is time for you to die to know
the joy of life, or you can take hold of it now and enjoy
the rest of your life.*

Onuma-sensei loved fishing, but he used to say that he
went fishing not so much to catch fish as to enjoy the sun
and the mountains, the fresh air, the birds in the sky and
the ducks on the surface of the water. He said that for him
fishing was a time to "not think"—to enjoy the subtle, ordinary moments of life. Unfortunately, few people take
time to do that. Most of us are so concerned with making
a living that we forget to live. We are like ducks swimming
along the surface of the water looking for nourishment
while a whole pond full of fish lies hidden below.

Health and Well-Being

When Onuma-sensei was young, tuberculosis was ram-
pant in Japan and he, like many of his compatriots, became dangerously ill with the disease. Later he was stricken
with a serious gallbladder problem. Luckily, he recovered
fully from these illnesses and went on to live a long, pro-
ductive life. But unlike many who have had similar serious illnesses Onuma-sensei refused to dwell on the fact
that all of us, all the time, are susceptible to illness and
accidents. Rather than sit back and contemplate his own
mortality, he used both experiences as catalysts to renew
his passion for kyudo. Onuma-sensei always credited his
love of the art for his return to good health, as well as
his continued health and well-being in later years. "The

practice of kyudo will add ten years to your life," he would say to anyone and everyone he met. This was the phrase he used when people commented that he looked and acted much younger than he was, or when potential students asked what benefit they could derive from the study of kyudo.

At first glance someone watching a kyudo demonstration might wonder what possible health benefits the practice might offer. To anyone accustomed to watching modern sports or gymnastics, the experienced kyudo practitioner appears to move in a slow, dreamlike state, expending little or no energy at all. But we can assure you that nothing could be further from the truth. Traditional Japanese archery is an extremely demanding form of physical exercise. Most beginners, even strong, athletic types, cannot pull and hold at full draw the bows used by experienced kyudo archers. We still have a memory of three burly European men who once attended a practice and were offended when Onuma-sensei gave them bows with a modest pull strength. After one of them asked Onuma-sensei—at the time, in his mid-seventies—what strength of bow he used, they insisted on being given bows of equal strength. He handed his own bow to the largest of the three, telling the man that if he could pull the bow to a full draw and hold it for a few seconds, all three men could use stronger bows. The man was unable to draw the bow, as were his friends after him. When the men then tried to draw the bows they had originally been given they found that these, too, proved extremely difficult to draw completely. Then, in a demonstration that left a lasting impression on all concerned, Onuma-sensei took each of their bows in hand and drew all three simultaneously. He stood there holding the three bows in full draw,

Deceptively simple in appearance, kyudo is in fact
demanding physical exercise

without a trace of apparent effort. Yet the combined pull
strength of the bows was more than twice that of his own.

When we asked how this was possible Onuma-sensei
explained that because the men were strong and muscular
they tended to rely on muscles alone to pull the bow.
"Blood and bone must be used in concert with the musculature to produce an effortless draw," we were told. His
explanation seemed simple enough: use the structural
strength of your entire body to pull the bow rather than
the muscles of the hands and arms alone. But we were
confused. What did he mean when he said to use the

blood? From the time we began our study he always said that we must practice technique until it melts into our blood and becomes a natural part of us. We deduced, therefore, that his deep familiarity with technique, in combination with the use of his musculature and skeletal structure, resulted in his effortless draw.

When we suggested this to him, he said we were on the right track, that technique was indeed important, but that his meaning was much simpler. He told us that the term "blood" literally referred to our circulatory system. To make an effort seem effortless we must discard all excess tension in our body. This improves our circulation and enables the body to absorb oxygen more efficiently from the lungs, in turn allowing us to slow our breathing rate. This helps keep the body relaxed and the mind calm, resulting in the most natural use of our physical and mental capabilities. To Onuma-sensei, the word "natural" suggests balance, since too much or too little of anything is unnatural. Insufficient or excessive physical or mental effort often leads to stress, exhaustion and a generally unhealthy life.

For Onuma-sensei kyudo was the perfect vehicle for creating balance in his life. He firmly believed that the concepts he learned from its practice were largely responsible for the blessings he enjoyed in life. He used the knowledge gained through training not only when shooting but in every aspect of his daily life: business, personal, even recreational. He once said that he had lost track of any distinction between the arts of kyudo and fishing, that both pastimes helped to keep him healthy and well. "To shoot well," he would say, "you must relax your body, correct your posture, control your breath and clear your mind. To fish well you must do the same." The same process can be applied to every other aspect of daily life as well. We are convinced that taking just a few moments from one's daily routine—whether at work, at home or at play—to release muscular tension, straighten the posture, calm the rhythm of the breath and clear the mind of unnecessary thoughts results in better mental and physical health.

Maintaining improved health and well-being requires our active, ongoing participation. Onuma-sensei always said that without our participation too much of life is left to chance. He once stood an arrow vertically in the palm of his hand to illustrate his point. If we do nothing, he said the arrow will fall randomly. But if we participate by gently moving the hand, we are able to keep the arrow balanced and exert a certain amount of control over its fate. To Onuma-sensei, vitality and mental sharpness were far too important to be left to chance.

Living a Full Life

When we speak of living a full life, this refers not to length but to quality. Most of us live marking time by various events—lunchtime, quitting time, bedtime; birthdays, holidays, weekends—and then wondering why our lives seem empty. We spend most of our time thinking not about where we are, but where we will be at some point in the future. Have you ever gone on a long-deserved holiday and in the middle of all the fun and relaxation found yourself thinking ahead to the day the trip will end? If so, you're not alone; this is common enough. But some people could be said to live their entire lives this way, always worrying about the day they will die.

Onuma-sensei liked to say life was like water flowing in a stream: it doesn't skip from stone to stone but flows

Onuma-sensei, shown here at age seventy-eight, credited kyudo with helping him look and feel years younger

unceasingly, touching everything in its path. To live a full life each of us must learn to appreciate each moment, and not just the high points. Onuma-sensei helped us to understand this better through the practice of kyudo, where we learned that every action has a beginning, middle and end, and that all are connected and equally important. A successful shot does not occur on its own, but is the result of the mental and physical components that preceded and followed the release of the arrow. One need not study kyudo to realize this. The artist knows that the stroke of ink or color left by a brush takes on meaning only when viewed in relationship to the strokes that went before and after. And to the musician, a note, no matter how beautiful, is not music except in the context of other notes. But perhaps more important is the knowledge that all these relationships have meaning only because of the interval that exists between them—the rest that connects the movement in kyudo, the space that surrounds the ink in painting and the intervals between notes that create harmony. Likewise, life has meaning only when we stop putting self-gratification first, and take the time to search for the beauty and subtlety present everywhere in our daily life.

◁ 3 ▷

In Search of the Self

There was a time when terms like "self-discovery" and "self-realization" were popular catchphrases. More recently, though, they have come to be seen as outmoded mantras of middle-aged former hippies. But the problem is not with the idea of self-discovery *per se*; it is with the "New Age" interpretation of it, which equates it with self-gratification. True self-discovery is a rewarding but completely unselfish experience that is not bounded by time or fashion.

Onuma-sensei thought of self-discovery as a "confrontation with the true self." He explained that each of us is given the opportunity several times a day to confront our true nature but that most of us are so absorbed in the day-to-day running of our lives that we fail to recognize this. Onuma-sensei said that every time we experience an outburst of emotion, perceive a slight against us or become irritated, this is a chance to turn inward and reflect on our true self. And if we notice that we react negatively in that kind of situation, we should immediately mark the moment and work on our character so that our reaction is more positive the next time around. Simply put, self-discovery is an essential step in self-improvement. It functions like a mirror, giving us an opportunity to see ourselves as we really are and to make necessary changes.

Fear, Fault and Responsibility

Most of us fear change because it can leave us feeling vulnerable and exposed. This can sometimes lead to moments of introspection and self-assessment, both of which can be painful. Not only must we suffer in that way, but then we can also sense that we are responsible for correcting any faults that may be revealed. Needless to say, it is much easier to find fault in others than in ourselves. So much so that in today's society a new subculture exists whose credo is, "I refuse to take responsibility for my actions because they are the result simply of a poor upbringing, bad education, wrongful society or whatever else I might choose to blame." Onuma-sensei used to say that perhaps the most difficult point in the study of kyudo was coming to terms with the fact that you alone are responsible for everything that happens. He once called our attention to a man who had a habit of examining his glove or bow after every poor shot. The man, of course, was trying to shift the blame from himself to, of all things, an inanimate object. Even supposing that the bow or glove was actually found to be defective, Onuma-sensei asked, would the problem be solved by glaring at them? Did the man expect the glove to feel shame and have itself repaired? Clearly it was the man's responsibility to attend to the care and maintenance of his personal equipment. Unfortunately his behavior is not unusual. Most of us have at one time or another taken out our frustration on inanimate objects, cursed them and thrown them down in

In this photo taken in Tokyo shortly after World War Two, U.S. servicemen practice Western archery alongside Japanese kyudo archers. The Allied forces banned all martial arts for a time, and Onuma-sensei was instrumental in having the ban lifted from kyudo

disgust. Given this tendency, then, it is easy to understand how people can so easily find fault in others while acknowledging very little in themselves. Someone once said that we hate in others what we most fear in ourselves. Could much of the violence in today's society be the result of such fear? Or the other way around: is hatred of others born of our fear of a people or culture different from our own? Onuma-sensei thought so. To his way of thinking, we fear most what we least understand.

Like any other country, Japan has its share of xenophobic individuals who dislike and distrust foreigners. Certainly there are those who believe that the arts and culture of Japan are incomprehensible to anyone but the Japanese themselves. But Onuma-sensei was not among them. The fact that we are writing this book is certain proof of that. Further, his openness and genuine friendship extended far beyond the two of us. Onuma-sensei had personal friends all over the world: from Australia to Iceland and nearly everywhere between. For the most part these were friends he had made through kyudo. He firmly believed that anybody, regardless of race, creed or culture, could learn the art of kyudo.

More importantly he believed that everyone, in spite of

Crucial training in shooting as a group

differences, is linked to everyone else. As individuals living together in a community of nations, we must take responsibility not only for the course of our own lives but for the direction of the whole of society as well; working in concert toward a common end without the need to fear or fault each other. His favorite example of this at work was in the group shooting procedure commonly used in kyudo practice where five individuals move together, separately but united—alternately standing, shooting and sitting—to complete the shooting ceremony. When this is done well it looks like one great, undulating organism in which the grace and elegance expressed by the individual components are magnified in the whole.

Truth, Goodness and Beauty

Of all the advantages that came from our close relationship with Onuma-sensei the most valuable was being able to return home with him after a lesson, sit down over a cup of tea and have a leisurely conversation. At those times he talked about a lot of things—some important, others not—but most significant for us was that he was open to questions that he did not always have time to elaborate on during regular practice. It was during those sessions that we discussed self-discovery with him:

> Sensei, you have often said that one of the objectives of kyudo practice is the search for the true self, but we have a friend who believes that people who are concerned with self-discovery are egotistical and selfish.
> *Self-discovery does not mean looking for characteristics peculiar to you alone; that certainly would be self-centered. True self-discovery means to search for characteris-*

tics that connect us to all other human beings. People have always sought to understand their humanity—to isolate and define the traits that separate us from other living things. Of course, we are blessed with a superior intellect, but what really sets us apart is our unlimited creative capacity. Many animals are builders and some can even fashion rudimentary tools, but humans alone are capable of conceptual creation. Science, philosophy, religion and art are all born from this ability. They are the products of our unique fascination with truth, goodness and beauty.

Truth, goodness and beauty are often mentioned in books on archery and by the teachers we meet.

Yes, the pursuit of these qualities is one of the most important elements of kyudo practice. Truth in kyudo is usually associated with the obvious; we equate true shooting with accurate shooting. Accuracy is, of course, important; since the ability to hit the target's center is basic to any form of archery. But kyudo makes a distinction between shooting that is merely skillful and shooting that is correct and right-minded. Because the Japanese bow is no longer used for hunting or war, though, and the target is nothing more than paper and wood, shooting simply for the sake of hitting the target seems rather meaningless in today's world. Kyudo addresses this problem by encouraging us to view the target as a reflection of our own strengths and weaknesses, and to use the shooting as a way to discover our true selves. That puts our competitive instincts to positive use, and gives the act of shooting deeper meaning. Sometimes we will hit the target but miss the self. At other times we will miss the target but hit the self. Our purpose, though, is to hit the target as the self, and hope that the sharp sound of arrow penetrating

The target is viewed as a reflection of one's own strengths and weaknesses

paper will awaken us from the "dream of life" and give us real insight into the ultimate state of being.

But not everyone studies kyudo. If truth is one of the qualities that links all human beings, and if it is essential in the discovery of our true selves, how will people who do not practice kyudo find truth?

As I said earlier, humans have created religion, science, art and philosophy to help them find truth, goodness and beauty. These qualities are certainly not found only through the practice of kyudo. Truth can be found in something as simple as a baby's cry. [Our infant son was crying at the time]

Now you've lost us.

[Sensei, laughing] *You will have to think about that one. But let's talk about goodness or beauty, they are easier to understand. Goodness is closely associated with the search for truth. And because it also includes qualities like courtesy, compassion, morality and nonaggression, almost everyone can agree on what it is. I know of no culture where immorality and aggression are considered good.*

What about war, where each side believes that it is right and just, and is fighting for the good of its people?

Yes, of course that happens. But there you've forgotten about truth. What is true for one side is not true for the other. Truth, goodness and beauty are all connected; you cannot have one without the others. Take kyudo practice, for example. When negative thoughts or actions enter into it, the mind becomes clouded and the shooting is spoiled, making it impossible to separate fact from falsehood. Anger, which is certainly not good, creates excessive tension in the body which makes for a forced release and poor shooting. If an arrow happens to hit the target, we will be unaware of the truth—that the shot was actually poor—simply because our mind and spirit were in a darkened state.

Beauty is more difficult to define because it varies greatly among different cultures and generations. I, for instance, may not always agree with you on what constitutes a beautiful painting, or what makes a woman beautiful. But we can all agree that beauty is something pleasant that enhances life and stimulates the spirit. In kyudo, beauty is most evident in the simple grace and artistry of the Japanese bow, or in the quiet elegance of the archer's attire. But the real beauty of kyudo lies else-

where. First of all, truth and goodness are themselves beautiful. In their absence kyudo is ignoble and vulgar. There is nothing uglier than a person who becomes so concerned with hitting the target or showing off his skill that he loses sight of the truth. Even worse is a corrupt and heartless person, because these qualities destroy all that is beautiful in kyudo. What I'm trying to say is that true beauty is not a surface quality; it is something that comes from within.

According to Onuma-sensei, then, kyudo is an excellent path in the search for truth, goodness and beauty, but it is by no means the only one. Just as each of us is given ample opportunity to confront our true nature, we are also given many occasions to find truth, goodness and beauty in our daily lives. These are provided by our family and friendships, our religion of choice, our work, recreation and surroundings, or in anything else that adds value and purpose to our lives. Truth, goodness and beauty are not rare qualities; they are elusive simply because so few people know how to find them. These qualities are revealed only when we expose the true self which we normally keep hidden behind the protective layers of the ego. Once we make an honest and thorough self-evaluation and begin to work to improve our character, we realize that our inability to understand ourselves colors our understanding of the rest of the world, and that the search for truth, goodness and beauty is really a search for that which we share with everyone else.

Three Stages of Self-Realization

There are three stages in one's search for the self: awareness, acceptance and perseverance. The biggest obstacle in our search is our lack of awareness. Many of us are searching for something, often without knowing just what. When asked, most would say they are looking for lasting love, happiness, inner peace or some similar state. All are admirable goals and all are attainable. Like truth, goodness and beauty these too are elusive only because we do not know how to search for them. Onuma-sensei once used the following analogy:

Imagine you have been told that a wonderful treasure exists at the end of a long and difficult journey. Excited by this knowledge you begin your quest for the treasure. It's not long before you find a small jewel lying on the path before you. It's beautiful but it's not the huge treasure you had heard about. Still determined, you toss it aside and go on with your search. As you continue along the path you find and toss away several other jewels of about the same size. Each is beautiful but you cannot be bothered with carrying around such small jewels when there is a much greater treasure in store. Finally, you reach the end of your journey and find that there is no great treasure waiting for you. Suddenly you realize that the treasure you were searching for was really nothing more than the accumulation of all the tiny jewels you found along the way—only now it is impossible to go back and retrieve them.

It is easy to adapt this story to so many of our lives. Substitute words like "love" or "friendship" for the words treasure and jewel and you tell the story of all the lonely people you ever knew. Change the words to "happiness" and you tell about misery and despair. It is indeed unfortunate that so many of us throw away love, friendship and

Onuma Hideharu with the authors' eldest son, Michael Hideharu DeProspero, in 1987

happiness simply because they fail to meet our expectations. Onuma-sensei tried to impress on us time and time again that everything we need for a joyful, fulfilling life is available to us now if we have eyes to see it.

It is easy, though, to focus on small details and lose sight of the whole. Practitioners of kyudo, for instance, often find themselves concentrating too hard on hitting the center of the target. The normal kyudo target is a series of concentric black circles on a white field, much smaller than the one commonly used in Western archery. When experienced practitioners miss the target, they tend to send the arrows to almost the same place each time. More often than not, the miss is but a hairsbreadth away from the target's edge. The interesting thing is that for special ceremonies very small targets, about the size of the center of a normal target, are used, and yet when they are missed, again the shot tends to sail just past the edge. One always comes away thinking that if everyone could shoot like that on the normal target, nobody would ever miss. When we first noticed this, we assumed it was a matter of correcting the aim but Onuma-sensei explained that the problem was not with technique but with the method of viewing the target. Focusing too intently on the target—its pattern, shape and size—narrows the field of vision and makes the target appear distant. As the perspective changes, the mind is drawn toward the target's periphery. The result is a shot aimed not at the target's center, but at its edge.

To help us overcome this problem Onuma-sensei taught us a simple exercise that eventually showed us how unaware we had become of our immediate environment and our place in it. He used a vase of multicolored flowers on his dining room table, but you may try the exercise using a photograph or painting, or any dense grouping of objects of different types and colors. At first he had us sit a short distance away from the flowers so that we could easily see the vase, flowers, table and surrounding objects. He then asked us to focus on a particular flower or leaf within the arrangement and stare at it for a moment or two, absorbing as much detail as possible. He asked us then to close our eyes and report on what we saw. If you try this, you should find that in the moments before the memory can retrieve the details, the mind first reconstructs the silhouette of the vase and flowers, devoid of all detail, and then adds the image of the specific flower or leaf you memorized. The remaining flowers, the vase and any other objects in your original field of view become insignificant to the memory and are, in essence, unseen. In this case of course the unseen constitutes the major part of the scene. Is this not how many of us spend much of our lives: absorbed in trivial concerns, having lost sight of the truly significant aspects of our existence?

But even after we become aware of the problem, why is it that we continue to let the mind sweep aside so much of what is important in life? We do this because awareness is only the first step in our search for self-realization. Anyone can—and many people will—tell you that you have a problem in your life, but until you accept this as a fact no change will occur in your behavior.

The second part of Onuma-sensei's exercise showed us a new way to look at our surroundings and helped us to accept the need for change on our part. The lesson continued with his telling us to look once more at the vase of flowers. This time, however, he instructed us not to set ourselves apart from the scene with our eyes fixed "flatly" on the flowers but to use our "mind's eye" to connect ourselves to the arrangement and its surroundings and see around, through and beyond it, adding depth and dimension, until it appeared to grow in size and move closer to us. He told us not to blink excessively or let our eyes dart around, but to take everything in, without fixing on any one element in particular.

This second instruction proved especially difficult for us. We found that the mind wanted desperately to attach itself to some part of the arrangement—to stop a moment and memorize an interesting shape or color. We felt that if it were not allowed to do this, we would not be able later to recall what we had seen. But Onuma-sensei urged us not to give in to this temptation. He assured us that the technique would ultimately increase our ability to see important details without sacrificing our ability to see the whole, and that it would add a new and exciting dimension to our practice of kyudo. Even though we were as yet unable to duplicate Onuma-sensei's way of seeing, and unsure that we would ever be able to do so, we knew in our hearts that his way was better than ours. Once we accepted that fact, we were ready to begin practicing the technique in earnest, and soon found that it was as difficult as we had suspected.

In truth we have yet to perfect the technique, but we were lucky enough, after many hours of practice under Onuma-sensei's direction, to eventually "see" the target grow in size and appear to come closer. But neither of us has been successful in consistently recreating the illusion since. However, we are grateful that he took the time to help us understand this way of seeing—we came away from the experience with a new awareness of not only the target but also our certain connection to it and our surroundings. As Onuma-sensei said about the phenomenon: "At that point there is no distance between man and target, man and man or man and universe—all are in perfect harmony."

That is where his teaching takes on significance outside of the shooting hall. We found that a heightened awareness of ourselves and our relationship with our surroundings—knowing what is and is not important in life—allows us to focus less on the day-to-day details of our existence and see that life, on the whole, is a gift so precious that we must treasure its every moment. We learned, too, that awareness must be accompanied by an acceptance of the existence of a problem. Once those two steps have been taken the only task remaining is perseverance: a personal commitment to stay the course until tangible results are obtained.

The ceremony marking the New Year. After Sensei offers blessings, each student will make a first shooting of the year

Onuma-sensei once likened his practice of kyudo to "a blind turtle in the middle of the ocean, searching for a log." He told us that sometimes he felt his situation was hopeless. He had studied so long, yet felt that he still knew so little. His study of kyudo, he said, required endless effort because there was no end to the obstacles he encountered. However, he found that if he persevered he always managed to break through them. "Once on the other side," he said, "things seem so clear and simple—I feel as if I can see further and wider than before." He emphasized that as long as we live we will have obstacles to overcome, but that these are a path to greater understanding of ourselves and so make all our effort worthwhile.

◁ 4 ▷

On Being Human

Onuma-sensei believed that one should strive constantly to be perfect. We talked about that one day over a cup of tea:

Sensei, what should our purpose be in studying kyudo?

To perfect ourselves.

Have you achieved perfection?

Of course not! It's not possible for humans to be perfect.

If it's impossible, then why try?

Because not to try is to be satisfied with being less than human.

Mankind's most precious gift is the gift of life, and each of us has a moral obligation to use it to explore the upper reaches of human potential. As Onuma-sensei once said, "Any animal can take from the earth what it needs to survive. Humans alone are obligated to put something back."

Facing Adversity

When we first began to study kyudo we knew we would face many challenges, but still we were unprepared for the obstacles that lay ahead. The equipment used in kyudo is primitive compared with that of Western archery. There are no mechanical accessories—sights, stabilizers or automatic release mechanisms—available to kyudo practitioners to compensate for human weakness. Consequently, when problems arise they generally cannot be solved by adjusting the equipment, but require that the archer make a more internal change. As a result, advancement in kyudo sometimes seems hopeless. If learning, in general, can be compared to climbing upward from one plateau to another, then learning kyudo must be likened to clambering over a sand dune, where any failure to move forward results in continual loss of ground. But Onuma-sensei assured us that the situation is never hopeless, provided we have the will to overcome our weaknesses. "Kyudo," he said, "is endless effort."

The same thing can be said of life itself. The struggle to survive is a never-ending process for any species, but this is perhaps especially true of humans. Of course, modern medical and scientific advances have greatly enhanced the quality of life, but mankind insists on turning its intelligence toward inventing new problems. As a result, the human race today faces difficulties that were unheard-of just a few generations ago. And unless we learn to temper our drive toward intellectual achievement with good judgment and common sense we should be prepared to face even greater adversity in the future.

On the one hand, being human makes us particularly vulnerable to the vicissitudes of life, but on the other it gives us a certain flexibility in our responses to them as

Kyudo is endless effort

well. This is where we differ from other living creatures: we may not be able to control events themselves, but we can control our reactions to them by recognizing that all of life's experiences, even unpleasant ones, conceal some positive lesson. To turn setback and disappointment into things of value, one need only look for these hidden lessons. Adversity need not break one's spirit, as it does with so many people. It has that power only because we become overwhelmed or lost in despair, and allow it to darken our outlook on life. In this state we can find no solutions. But solutions do exist. We need only to remember that and endlessly seek them.

When Opinions Differ

When we were younger, we thought that there must be a way for humans to learn to get along with one another.

We once asked Onuma-sensei if he didn't think that kyudo would be a perfect catalyst for that kind of change. His answer, an uncharacteristically terse "No," so surprised us that we let the topic drop. Later, though, we decided to pursue it further. This was our conversation:

> At one point we were confident that the world was going to be a better place for the next generation. But nowadays it begins to seem that the human race is doomed to constant bickering. Not that people are content with this situation: for centuries they have looked to theology, philosophy, astrology and other methods for solutions, generally with little success. Once, in an earlier conversation, we asked if you thought that kyudo could help make things fundamentally different for human beings and you said no. Do you still feel that way?
>
> *Kyudo is no better or worse than other ways to effect change. It is just one of many methods, and the number of kyudo practitioners is minuscule in comparison with other methods, like religions.*
>
> But that's precisely why kyudo could work, because too many people in today's world are disillusioned with religion. Religion is supposed to be about peace, harmony and acceptance of others, but instead it seems to be the cause of much of the discord in the world today.
>
> *And you think all this could be changed if people studied kyudo?*
>
> Well, you said that kyudo has taught you a lot about yourself and helped you to make many changes in your life.
>
> *That's true. But that doesn't mean it can change the world.*

But you always tell us that harmony is a major element of kyudo practice. Maybe if everyone studied kyudo there would be less disagreement in this world. *Only if everybody studied under the same teacher. Even then, agreement among people would only last for a short while. Eventually someone would come out with a new or slightly unique interpretation of a teaching and this would sow the seeds of disagreement. If the disagreement is great enough the group splits into two discordant groups whose members attempt to convert others to their specific way of thinking. Of course this is the same thing that happens in many religions. You see, it doesn't matter whether it is kyudo, religion or any other method a person may use, the cycle will continue as long as we dwell on the outward form and ignore the underlying concepts.*

Later, in other conversations, Onuma-sensei explained that when we are searching for something to believe in we are attracted first to the message: to concepts that coincide with the particular set of beliefs we already have in place. We meet others who think similarly and begin to associate with them: humans are social animals and take great comfort being in the company of others, especially others of like mind. However, as a group matures, so does individual opinion. People begin to focus less on the message—on which they may still be in complete agreement—and more on the method of communicating the message to others. That is, their attention shifts from the concepts that originally drew them together to individual teaching techniques. Unfortunately, once this happens it is not long before the concepts themselves are lost amid differences of opinion on how to teach them. Subsequent generations, who are drawn to the method of study by the concepts, find that these have been overwhelmed by technical questions. Disheartened, they look elsewhere, only to be discouraged again and again.

Is there any way to break this cycle? Onuma-sensei thought there was: seeing and accepting how closely each of us is related to all other human beings. To help us visualize this relationship he once asked us to look at a bowl of tangerines. When scrutinized carefully, each was unique, but all were tangerines nonetheless. He then peeled the skin away from several tangerines to make them more uniform. Finally he broke them into individual sections and dumped them back in the bowl, asking us to identify which sections belonged to which peel. Of course, we could not say.

Onuma-sensei said that humans are like the tangerines. We think of ourselves as unique because of our dissimilar outer traits, yet on the inside we are very much the same. We also divide our thoughts and ideas into small sections—labeling them truth, knowledge, reality, religion or whatever—and believe that these too add to our uniqueness. But when all our ideas are spread out before us are they not like the tangerine sections in the bowl, he asked, basically indistinguishable?

Discord arises not when people have different opinions, but when they try to force their opinions on others. Forcing an opinion on another person implies a lack of respect for his opinion or even for him as a person. According to Onuma-sensei, a constructive relationship between two people is like the relationship between an archer and a bow. "The nature of the bow is to resist your pull," he said. "It is designed to do the opposite of what you are trying to do. If you do not respect the bow's nature, but try to force it to follow your wishes, the result will be a disastrous shot. The same is true of people. Even if someone's opinion is totally opposed to your own there is always good reason to listen to it carefully and try to understand the thinking behind it. No one can know everything, and if you should fail to understand another's point of view there is a good chance that you may have overlooked something important."

Do you agree? If not, let's find something everyone can agree on. Imagine a coin—just a normal, round coin. If we ask a hundred people to describe its shape, all will agree that it is circular. It's not rectangular, square or triangular. Everyone agrees and life is easy. But then someone comes along and says, "You know, I think it is rectangular." Suddenly there is disagreement. The person is clearly ignorant. How can he disagree with such an overwhelming consensus? One common reaction is to ridicule and belittle a wayward opinion or even to reject the person who holds it.

But what if, instead, we took the time to try to understand this opinion? What would make a person believe that a coin is rectangular? To find the answer we could consider the places where coins are used and remember that these include, for instance, public telephones and vending machines. Naturally, the coin slot in these devices is rectangular. Therefore, one might assume that a coin must also be rectangular. And so it is, more or less, when held sideways. Oddly enough, a coin can be both circular and rectangular. To recognize this, it is necessary to entertain the possibility that another point of view might be valid. People who cannot do this limit their own possibilities for development, since tolerance of differing opinions is essential to the evolution of human knowledge.

Human Relationships

We may speak of people's interconnectedness, but this does not imply that humans lack individuality. What a sad, boring world this would be if all of us were the same. Even Japan, which prides itself on its homogeneous culture, is in truth a nation of individuals. Japanese may show common physical traits and hold certain shared beliefs, but all in all their personal identities are no less unique as people's anywhere else. This is in fact summed up in the Japanese proverb *Junin to-iro* ("ten men, ten colors"). And of course there's nothing wrong with having a unique personal identity—personal identity, after all, helps us establish a sense of self-worth—but when that identity begins to overshadow the identity of others, when self-worth gives way to conceit, we lose sight of the human connection. That causes us to see anyone different from us in a negative light. Instead of focusing on differences it is more fruitful to look for the similarities that exist between all human beings.

As an example let's consider the relationship between men and women. In any country and in any culture, this is one of the readiest ways to underscore the difference between human beings. Onuma-sensei once cautioned that women should not try to shoot like men. And because Japanese men are notorious for their sexist thinking, we supposed that perhaps his comment was a reflection of such beliefs. But we were wrong. The following conversation with Onuma-sensei reveals a person able to see beyond obvious individual differences and find the characteristics that are common to all:

> Sensei, you have said that women should not try to shoot like men. Do you mean that kyudo is different for men and women?

The authors practice at the Toshima-ku Kyudojo

[Sensei, laughing] *I think maybe these days any answer I give will get me in trouble. No, what I mean is that there are certain natural differences between men and women that must be respected. Women are blessed with a grace and beauty that is lacking in most men. Also, they are less prone to resort to the use of excessive strength. Therefore women should take advantage of these qualities and not try to imitate men who, for their part, must learn to be more graceful and use less strength. On the other hand, being too weak is also not good. I guess there is a point of balance between men and women that is neither too rigid nor too weak. That's what we must all search for.*

It sounds like you are saying that men should be more like women and vice versa.

No, men should be men and women should be women. There are some differences that must be respected, such as biological limitations, but most other human characteristics are shared by both sexes. Restrictions of a culture or society might cause a sex to accentuate or suppress certain of those characteristics, but they all exist nevertheless. The truth is that humans—men and women of all cultural backgrounds—are more alike than they care to admit. If they concentrated more on seeking those similarities there might be a lot less division in the world.

This exchange prompted us to recall an incident that happened to us in the early days of our stay in Japan. A new building was being erected in our neighborhood and we were forced to walk past the construction site every morning and evening on our way to work and home again. What made the trip unusual for us was the construction worker posted there as guard, whose role it was to help passersby navigate the narrow walkway in front of

At the 1987 cherry blossom festival in Washington, D. C.

the building. The route was clear and not at all dangerous, so the guard was not really necessary, but he was there anyway, to politely remind us to watch our step. At the same time he would apologize for all the noise and inconvenience caused by the building's construction.

We remembered thinking that similar scenes used to take place in America twenty or thirty years ago but seemed almost nonexistent today. When we mentioned this to an American friend he scoffed that such customs are meaningless attempts by the Japanese to create enough work for everyone in their society. He explained that in America it would not be practical to hire a "courtesy guard" to patrol construction sights.

Perhaps he is right. But we also remember how good it felt to pass by the site each day and be on the receiving

Onuma-sensei speaks with guests at a kyudo demonstration in Washington, D. C.

end of the guard's courteous remarks, whatever the reason for them. When we mentioned our friend's reaction to Onuma-sensei, he noted that cultural differences are often a cause of confrontation but that such confrontations need not occur if we learn to respect other cultures. He recalled that he had experienced countless similar instances of courtesy on his travels throughout the world and was convinced that even though societies change over the years, basic human nature remains the same.

Human Behavior

Most living species rely on instinct to survive. For them, to kill is to live. Our ancestors once lived by a similar code so each of us still carries the remnants of such behavior deep inside, but over the ages humans have developed other, more sophisticated characteristics that insulate us from the kill-or-be-killed principle. There is no morality in nature; the predator feels no hatred for its prey, nor any shame at having killed. There is no victor or victim; these are human concepts that have no meaning for a hungry animal.

Unlike other living species, humans are blessed with the ability to reflect on the consequences of their own behavior. Modern society has come to accept certain standards of what constitutes right and just human behavior. Nearly every society bans senseless and random killing of other humans. This kind of ban takes on renewed importance in technologically advanced societies that have developed, with nuclear capacity, the power to wipe out every living species on the planet with the touch of a button.

But if we are agreed that might does not necessarily equal right, why do we allow the strong to continue to prey on the weak? Is it because we do not care? That isn't the way it should be. As Onuma-sensei used to say, "Even a hunter will not harm an injured bird that flies under his coat for protection." In our opinion, a civilized society is one that cares for its weakest members. Could it be, then, that we allow the strong to prey on the weak because we have a warped perception of what real human strength is? True strength is not physical; nor is it the product of wealth, power or position. It comes only when we aspire to help, and never hurt, those less fortunate than ourselves. The bully at school may be big and strong, but he preys upon weaker children because he himself is weak at heart. The criminal who shoots and kills an unarmed victim demonstrates his impotence, not his virility. And when politicians use their power for personal gain at others' expense, this is a sign of moral weakness and not of strength of will.

Part of human behavior is innate but the greater part is

Onuma-sensei performs *monomi*, or sending his spirit to make contact with the target before beginning the shooting sequence

learned. Our perceptions of strength and weakness are just two of the many things we learn from observing the way our parents and other adults behave. Yet how many generations have grown up being advised to "Do as I say, not as I do"? What a meaningless thing to say when you are trying to instill values in a child. Anyone who has spent time around children knows that they learn best by example. The cycle of one generation complaining about the values of the next will continue forever unless we stop right now, reflect on what it means to be human and examine our own behavior so that we can pass on only the best examples to our children.

Author with his daughter Mika in 1993 at Toshima-ku Kyudojo

Onuma-sensei liked to remind us that each of us carries genes from our primitive ancestors who fought and killed one another to survive, but that we also carry, alongside those, the potential for enlightenment. "You can yield to the call of your ancestors and lead a miserable life with a darkened spirit," he sometimes said, "or aspire to be a perfect human being and be rewarded with an illuminated spirit—one that is bright and positive and that embodies the very best in human nature."

◁ 5 ▷

Teaching and Learning

Onuma-sensei began the study of kyudo as a young boy of seven and practiced the art until his death at the age of eighty, giving him more than seventy years' experience. We, on the other hand, began to study kyudo under him less than fifteen years ago. Onuma-sensei liked to compare one's term of study with the passage from infancy to adulthood: the knowledge that we gain from our period of study is equivalent to the experience we acquire in all of life. If that is the case, then throughout our period of study with him we were nothing more than confused children trying to make some sense of the teachings of a wise old man. Be that as it may, we learned more from Onuma-sensei in the short time we studied with him than we ever have from any other teacher. He taught us more than kyudo: he taught us the arts of teaching and learning.

Learning anything new is difficult. This is especially true for adults who must endure embarrassing situations and fumble with awkward techniques as they struggle to acquire new information and skills. Given a choice, most

83

adults would rather forgo gaining a new skill than suffer through the learning process. Young children, on the other hand, struggle less. They get so excited about the process and the prospect of learning that they let nothing get in their way. "The secret of a successful learner," said Onuma-sensei, "is to become like a child again. And the secret of a successful teacher is to see through the eyes of the learner."

The Teacher's Art

We have observed that for many of today's teachers teaching is no longer a profession, but a job like any other. How many parents complain that their children are not receiving the education they need to get by in life? Real teaching means real involvement with each student; something that is increasingly difficult in modern classrooms where a single teacher is responsible for the education of thirty or more pupils. But how many parents are willing to pay more taxes to train and hire more teachers and build better schools? Very few, it seems; funding for educational programs continues to decline in communities across the United States, with little sign of a reversal likely in the near future. Should teachers throw up their hands in despair, show up for work each day, collect their paycheck at the end of the month and blame it all on the parents and politicians? That is not the answer if they pride themselves on being real teachers. Teaching is an art and art does not come easy.

When an artist paints a canvas he or she does not separate the process into individual components: in a good painting, artist, canvas, medium and technique are all equally important. Likewise a good teacher cannot separate the act of teaching from the process of learning. A teacher who thinks only of teaching and being a teacher separates himself from the learner. And a teacher who has forgotten what it is like to learn has never really discovered how to teach. Like any artist, a good teacher must constantly strive to know and perfect his craft. A mediocre grasp of the art of teaching and an unclear purpose result in mediocre lessons and disinterested students.

Watching Onuma-sensei teach was like watching a master artist paint. As soon as he met a prospective student he made a rough mental sketch of the person's skills and, more important, aptitude. He then laid down the foundation for training—the fundamental moves and techniques that would later form the basis of the person's shooting style. For the most part, the foundation for one student was the same as that for the next, but there were subtle differences—shadings, if you will—that hinted at the

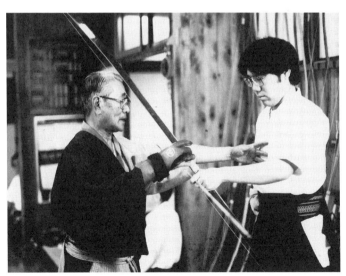

Onuma-sensei instructs a young student

direction he was planning to take with a particular pupil. The differences might be in the way Sensei emphasized various mental, physical or spiritual elements of the training—each according to a student's needs. And when a student continued to practice for months or years, it was possible to watch his natural talent developing along the lines that Onuma-sensei had sketched out.

No two people are alike and of course no two students are, either. We had not been studying long when we noticed that Onuma-sensei taught different students differently. Once we had established a trusting relationship with him, after a few years of practice, we asked why his teaching style showed so much variation from one student to another when the practice of kyudo, in terms of both shooting procedure and technique, was basically the same for everyone:

Sensei, we've noticed that you don't always teach the same things to every student. With some people you are very actively involved in the learning process and you give a good deal of personal attention. But you leave other students to practice by themselves a lot of the time. Is this because you like some students more than others?

[Sensei, laughing] *No, of course not. A teacher must treat all students equally as people—remember that, because it's very important—but it's not true that all people are equal as students. There are many reasons why I teach people differently. It may be that a particular student needs more attention—or less, as the case may be. Also, people learn at different rates, so some students are ready to progress to the next stage of training before others. But perhaps the biggest reason is that, although they may come to my class to learn, some students are not actually ready to accept my teaching. In most cases they are so filled with their own ideas—what kyudo is, how to practice it, how to teach it—that I must stand aside and give them time to decide which concepts are more important for their progress: the old ones they brought with them to the training hall or the new ones I am trying to teach them. Teaching students like that is like trying to paint a new picture over an old one: it's not impossible but it's difficult. The very best students only need to be told something once. They're like blank sheets of paper— open and ready to accept the information that is presented to them.*

Both of you are teachers but you work at a private school where all the students pay an equal amount of money to attend your classes. For that reason you think that you have to be fair and teach everyone in exactly the same way. But I get no money for my teaching: I do not recruit students and I do not chase after those who wish to leave. I do not teach a group of people; I teach individuals. It may appear on the surface that I am ignoring some student and focusing on another but that is never the case. I am very much aware of the wishes of every one of my students. But I teach each according to their needs, not their wants. This may seem cold, but it is a teacher's responsibility to lead students in the right direction.

It is the teacher's job to encourage students to take an active part in the learning process. Occasionally it is necessary for a teacher to tell a student that something is right or wrong, but most of the time the student should be made to seek the answer for themselves. In the search for knowledge the student is the explorer, and the teacher the

guide. Books, computers and other teaching aids are useful but they can never replace the traditional one-to-one
relationship between teacher and student. Unfortunately,
that kind of relationship is fast succumbing to the pressures of modern education: overcrowded classrooms and
fewer full-time instructors. The general trend today is to
pack as many students into the room as possible, lecture
them, distribute reading material and assign a lot of
homework in the hope that people will memorize at least
part of the information included in the day's lesson. But
does anyone honestly believe that works? Think back to
your favorite teachers, the ones you remember as having
given you something worthwhile. We would bet that not
one was the kind of teacher who stood in front of the
class giving straight lectures or exams based solely on
memorization.

A teacher who simply hands out information is one
who has forgotten what it's like to learn. Teachers of that
sort have forgotten the curiosity, the wonder, that goes
hand-in-hand with discovery. They have grown inflexible,
and that makes them incapable of seeing anything outside
of their own frame of knowledge—or even anything outside their lesson plan. Take the case of our eldest son,
Michael, as an example. When he was in second grade his
teacher was discussing the differences between gases and
liquids. She explained that you can touch a liquid such as
water, and feel it on your hand, but that you cannot touch
a gas such as air. Our son said that he could indeed feel
air, and demonstrated by waving his hand vigorously. His
teacher remarked that she did not mean that, she meant
that you could not hold air the way you could hold water.
Michael thought about that for a moment and said he
could also hold air. He took a deep breath and held the

air in his puffed-out cheeks. Her response to his evident delight with his own answers was to insist that he did not understand. Later, when Michael related the story to us, he started crying and asked why his teacher wouldn't listen to him. We could only suggest that perhaps she was behind schedule and didn't have time to explore other possibilities. This may even have been true, but rather than dampen his curiosity we are convinced that she should have taken a moment to applaud his efforts and to encourage him to study the matter further. Certainly, the time that would take would not be enough to disrupt an entire lesson; but it might well be enough to instill a life-long passion for learning in a student.

Apathy and insensitivity on the part of a teacher can destroy a student's will to learn, but an overly zealous teacher can sometimes be just as bad. Onuma-sensei warned us not to over-teach. He believed that too many instructors like to impress students with their own knowledge rather than impart knowledge to the students. They become so engrossed in minute, often inconsequential, detail that they overwhelm the students' ability to reason and to comprehend the lesson. Onuma-sensei used to say, "That's like trying to improve the health of a cow by straightening its horns. You only end up killing the cow." What he meant was that before you attempt to solve a problem, be sure your solution is going to work. By forcing a student to absorb a great deal of information at one sitting you make it less likely that they will retain any important information at all.

We have a simple exercise we often use to demonstrate how hard it is to learn when someone over-teaches. In the exercise we tell the student that we are going to teach him to forge our signature. A signature is deeply personal; it is something that you alone have refined over the course of many years. Teaching someone else to imitate it is not an easy task—nor necessarily a good idea—but you need not worry about forgery, since you can make it impossible to learn by teaching it this way:

> Tell the student to follow your strokes as you begin to write your signature, but as he attempts to do so give him a steady stream of corrections on points like the amount of pressure he should apply at the beginning, middle and end of a stroke; the length or angle of the lines; the arc of the curves; the circumference of the loops. If your student is too faithfully recreating the strokes, you can still criticize that too. Let no mistake pass without a detailed lecture on what a correct signature should look like. If you want to be particularly "helpful" you can always grab hold of his hand and make the corrections for him as he passively follows along.

On the other hand, if you want to teach well you just need to remember that there is more to it than keeping people preoccupied with information and technique. In order to really learn, a student must be helped to see in new ways. To do this he must be confronted with ideas at odds with his own. A good teacher should even be willing to set aside his ego and temporarily take a position contrary to his own beliefs, if that will help a student understand. Naturally, such contradictions cause the student some doubt and confusion, but the combination of doubt and confusion generates insight in the same way that flint and iron combine to make fire.

A good teacher must never forget that just as an infant

Watching Onuma-sensei draw the bow

cannot ingest large portions of food, the beginning student can't process complex thoughts or techniques. Yet the teacher must not let the student feel that a lesson is easy. Every lesson must be challenging, but never daunting, and presented in a way that allows the student to acquire enthusiasm for the learning process, respect for the teacher and self-confidence. As Onuma-sensei said: "When you teach, you give a lot and you take away a lot, but if you take away the learner's confidence you take away all desire to learn."

The Art of Learning

Every teacher has had his share of students who have difficulty learning. Good teachers will first look to their own approach for the source of the problem. But there are cases in which a teacher has done everything possible to help a student understand, and still the student fails to learn. At that point it's important to remember that no teacher, not even a great one, can succeed if a student doesn't have a sincere desire to learn. It's also important to remember that the desire to learn is an innate human characteristic: when it is lost there must be some reason.

Generally speaking, students lose the desire to learn for lack of one of three things: inspiration, realism or focus. The uninspired student does not believe in the teacher; nor, as a result, does he believe in himself. This student has low self-esteem and few or no goals in life, and is content to learn only what is needed to get by in daily life. The unrealistic student expects far too much of himself. He sets unrealistic goals and is disheartened when he fails to reach them. For him, the idea of losing is so distasteful that he would rather not try than risk failure. Finally, the unfocused student is not clear about how to learn. He knows learning is important but he is unsure of his own role in the process. This is the kind of student who is labeled a "lazy learner" for preferring to sit back and be taught rather than take an active part.

For all three types of students, learning to learn becomes as important as learning to teach is for the teacher. To help us learn kyudo, Onuma-sensei gave us some simple guidelines to follow. Here are some that we believe can help any learner in any situation:

• *Always strive to do your best. Never accept mediocrity in yourself.*
In kyudo we are taught that any shot, even one that is seemingly perfect, can be improved because all human beings—in mind and spirit—have unlimited potential for improvement. Never accept from yourself, or from others, the idea that you are unable to learn. With continued efforts and the will to succeed you can learn as much as, or more than, the next person.

• *Be flexible and open-minded. Resist the temptation to reject any teaching that does not coincide with your own opinions and preconceptions.*
Never limit your choices by making prior decisions about what you wish to learn. Take for example the man—who shall remain nameless—who as a young high school student was encouraged by his teachers to take a typing class as an elective course. But this student was interested only in art and chose instead to take a study period so he could practice his drawing. He was happy enough until, years later, he found himself in sore need of typing skills as he

struggled to write a book about his teacher. His story has a happy ending only because he was fortunate enough to have married a woman who had learned how to type.

• *Learn to study on your own. Your instructor can show you the way, but you must make an equal effort to learn.*
Onuma-sensei said over and over that the teacher is the guide and the student is the explorer. Along these same lines he once told us that good teachers are like the giant drums displayed at Shinto shrines. They make no sound until they are struck. This does not mean that teachers should become passive or lazy. It means that teaching and learning are a shared experience; the teacher is there to help the student, but the student cannot sit back in silence and hope to learn. He must "sound out" the teacher as he would a drum.

• *Listen and watch. Do not expect to be actively taught all the time. Learn to "steal" from the teacher by observing and copying the way he does things.*
Onuma-sensei liked to say, "The highest form of teaching is not to teach at all." His words echo the Japanese saying, "A child living near the temple learns sutras without being taught." The thinking behind these sayings is that people learn by imitating others. This is the most natural way to learn. It requires more patience, sensitivity and awareness than does book learning but its rewards are greater.

• *Never make excuses when you don't understand. If you're confused, go back to the basics. They are the ideal place to make a fresh start.*

Everyone gets confused when learning something new, so there is no shame in admitting that a lesson is difficult and that you are confused. It's far better to ask a teacher to explain something again from the beginning than to waste time pretending you understand. Excuses are a way of buying time when we are embarrassed by failure to understand. But all they do is take time away from real learning.

• *Don't be afraid of failure. See it as a learning experience that provides an opportunity for continued growth.* Once, after we'd failed several tests in succession, Onuma-sensei commented that we were lucky because we learn a little when we pass a test, but we learn a lot more when we fail. "Feel pity," he said, "for people who have never failed, because their commitment to learn has never been challenged." To develop a deeper understanding of any subject you must test your own ideas and assumptions every so often. Failure gives you the chance to do just that.

Above all, the art of learning requires that we see with "new eyes." That means that before we can learn anything new we must first learn to look at familiar surroundings in a new way. The best way to do this is to see through the eyes of the teacher, but this requires trust, patience and perseverance because the experienced teacher often sees in ways that are totally unfamiliar to us. Here it is important to remember Onuma-sensei's analogy about the best students being like a blank sheet of paper—open and ready to accept information. The following exercise will demonstrate how much easier it is to learn when the mind is relatively free of preconceptions:

You will need two dissimilar pictures or photographs and a blank, preferably white, sheet of paper. First, lay the blank sheet on the table directly in front of you, and then pick up one of the pictures. Look carefully at the picture for a few moments, paying close attention to its shape, color and design. When you're ready, put the picture aside and immediately look at the blank paper. You should find it easy to project a mental image of the picture, whether on the blank sheet or just in front of it. Now set aside the blank sheet and lay the first picture down on the table within easy reach. Pick up the second picture and study it as you did the first. Take as much time as you like, then put it aside and pick up the first picture. Try to recreate the second image on top of the first. Most people find this very difficult to do.

Leonardo da Vinci's Mona Lisa, as seen through a cylinder

With repeated practice you may be able to combine the two images, but even if you should manage it, can you ever be sure where one image begins and the other ends? In the same way, can a student whose mind is filled with preconceptions ever see what a teacher sees? The problem is that a student's preconceptions are often founded on misconceptions; this makes teaching that much harder. Onuma-sensei said this kind of student is like someone who looks at a beautiful painting through a cylinder. He sees only a small portion of what is really there so he tries to imagine what the rest of the painting looks like. When this happens real ideas are replaced by symbols—the representation of ideas.

Symbolic representations of a star, a tree and a house

If we asked you to draw a star, a tree and a house would they look like the drawings shown above? If so, then in your own mind you may have replaced stars, trees or houses with the symbols for those objects. We are willing to bet you have never seen a real star, tree or house that looked anything like the ones you've just depicted. And a more honest rendering doesn't require great talent. The drawings below were done by our children. In spite of their naiveté the drawings reflect what the children

A star, a tree and a house, as drawn by Michael and Mika DeProspero

actually saw and experienced, not what they imagined. We do not mean to suggest here that imagination is unimportant; imagination, after all, is a vital element in the creative process. But creativity is not learned—it is revealed only when the analytical mind is quieted and intuitive thought processes take over. Teachers can give students the opportunity to experience creativity, but they can't show students how to be creative.

Fortunately, most of what a teacher knows is teachable—and learnable—but it takes patience on the part of the learner. Lack of patience is probably the learner's biggest challenge. An experienced teacher's knowledge of a subject is vast and complex. It is like a movie that runs continuously in his mind. He knows the movie backward and forward, including every character and every word of dialogue. The student, on the other hand, knows very little, perhaps only the title of the film or a brief plot summary. For the sake of the student the teacher is forced to break down his knowledge into small, easily understandable fragments—or frames of the movie, if you will. If a student is to learn, he must be attentive for long periods of time. This provides the continuity between the frames of the movie.

Could anyone understand a movie while running in and out of the theater, watching only a few frames at a time? To compensate for what he had missed the person would try to fill in the gaps with information gathered from his own experiences. And that would totally alter the content of the film. Unfortunately, many students do just this. They seek knowledge, but they become easily bored and quit or move on to another teacher when learning does not come as easily or as fast as they'd like. Onuma-sensei called these *ka-deshi* (mosquito students) since they

In a time-honored tradition, kyudo technique is passed from one generation to the next

are only around for a short time each year. Like their namesakes, mosquito students are noisy; they complain constantly that they're not being taught. What they fail to understand is that their own impatience makes them difficult to teach.

Learning and teaching are twin arts with a single purpose: passing knowledge on from one source to another. Student and teacher are equally responsible for that happening. As Onuma-sensei said, "It is the teacher's responsibility to teach and the student's responsibility to learn." When the process is unsuccessful, neither side should blame the other. Both should simply go back to the basics, and remind themselves how to go about studying or teaching. Only then will the process be complete.

◁ 6 ▷

Work and Responsibility

One dictionary defines "work" as the effort to produce or accomplish something, and "responsibility" as the condition of being able and ready to meet one's obligations. But to Onuma-sensei, work and responsibility were one and the same; he made no distinction between them. Work is something we all must do. Whether it be at schoolwork, housework, social work or hard work, each of us has an obligation to put forth our best efforts to accomplish something of value. The English author Samuel Butler said, "Every man's work, whether it be literature or music or pictures or architecture or anything else, is always a portrait of himself." We are defined, in part, by the work we do. But, more importantly, we are also defined by the way we do our work. Not everyone has a choice in the work they do. Socioeconomic factors in combination with educational opportunities often determine our status in the work force. But all of us, from street cleaner to corporate president, have a choice about the way we do our work. We can be diligent and meticulous and strive for unequaled quality, or we can be lazy and negligent, content to produce mediocre results.

Advanced instructors at Toshima-ku Kyudojo ready their bows

The Worker's Responsibility

"Whatever is worth doing at all, is worth doing well." These words of Lord Chesterfield's were one of Onuma-sensei's favorite Western sayings. If there was one thing he repeatedly tried to teach us it was that every human being has a responsibility to pursue excellence in every phase of his existence. He made that clear from our very first lesson, when he remarked that before learning anything about kyudo we had better learn the correct way to take off our shoes and enter the training area. He was not being a stickler for proper shoe care; he was trying to instill in us from the very beginning a sense of the importance of striving for quality in thoughts and actions.

Onuma-sensei believed every human being had a responsibility to pursue excellence

He once told us that he always watched the way that prospective students behaved when they were not shooting. People who were careless with their own equipment or with that of others and people who were sloppy in their manner or dress struck him as having little regard for the importance of quality in life. He maintained that while few may be born into the higher stations of life, all of us—regardless of social order, community, class or profession—are born with the ability to think and act with a high degree of excellence. All we need, he believed, is to be taught from early on that excellence is its own reward.

Here is a conversation we once had with him on the subject:

When we were kids we were taught to always put our best effort into a project. But it seems that young people today have no desire to excel in anything. We are not that old; how could things change so drastically in such a short period of time?

Maybe it is because young people today have learned that their efforts will not be respected. You're both teachers. Which do you see more often in your school—teachers who constantly criticize and complain about students' inability to understand, or those who take time to guide and nurture students who are having trouble?

We have to admit that the latter type is rare.

And you're parents now. You see other parents. Which do you think is more prevalent—parents who are patient with children and help them learn, or parents who ignore and punish children instead of taking time with them?

We see your point, but what about adults who have mediocre work habits and who are unconcerned with the quality of the work they produce? You can't send them back to their parents and teachers to be reeducated.

No, but adults can reeducate themselves. If they have no concern for quality in their lives it is because they have never learned what quality is. Quality is the same as excellence, but many people confuse excellence with superiority. When I speak of excellence I am not talking about the belief that one is superior to others because of a particular talent for one thing or another. To my way of thinking that is not excellence, but arrogance. To me, excellence is being the very best in everything—not only in what you do, but in what you think and say.

Author with his son Michael in 1993

In a later conversation Onuma-sensei said that society would work much better if everyone took a little time to reexamine his own commitment to excellence. All anyone expects of you is your best. Your parents expect you to be the best person you can be; your teachers expect you to learn as much as possible; your employer expects you to do the best work that you know how. These are not unreasonable expectations, so why do they pose such a challenge for so many people? One reason may be that some people expect extra compensation for extra effort. Children expect a reward from their parents for doing good, students expect praise from teachers for learning something new, and employees expect praise or even bonuses from the company for producing something of quality. But these are people who never learned that excellence is its own reward. It may be a well-worn phrase but there is still a great deal of truth in it. Doing your best at home, at school or at work brings rewards in the form of smoother family relationships, better understanding between student and teacher and less conflict between employer and employee.

It would seem that avoiding conflict with an employer would be ample reward for anyone since the employer, unlike a parent or teacher, can terminate the relationship at any time if they are not pleased with the work being done. A worker is hired for both his ability and his potential. The employer asks only that a worker work to the best of his ability while trying to fulfill his potential. That is every worker's responsibility. In return the employer compensates him with financial and other benefits. That is the employer's responsibility. We have been in both positions at different times and our biggest headache, as an employer, was getting a good day's work from some of our staff. We always wondered how anyone could work so hard to get a job—filling out the resumé and applications, sitting through the interviews—then work so little once hired. It often seemed that some employees spent more time trying to get out of work than actually working. That we were successful at all was due only to a couple of core employees who did twice the work to compensate for others' inadequacies.

We once mentioned this problem to Onuma-sensei but he just seemed puzzled. He maintained that in Japan they did not have that problem. According to him, Japanese employers and employees usually enjoy a more cooperative relationship, with both sides very much aware of their responsibilities. Employees know that if they do their very best at all times their employers will be pleased, there will be less friction in the workplace and the company will run more smoothly and efficiently. As a result they know that they will be rewarded not only with financial security but also with pleasant working conditions that will make the jobs seem less like work.

If this seems a little too much to expect from an employee outside of Japan consider this: we have a friend who is a successful businessman in the United States. Recently, however, he commented that increasing competition and rising costs are making it more and more difficult for him to keep his businesses profitable. Even after extensive research he and his management team were hard-pressed to come up with any other measures to improve performance. Of course, there was always the option of cutting costs by reducing the work force or by limiting employee benefits, but our friend was known for his fair and sympathetic treatment of employees and he refused to even consider that alternative. The only area

Soon after the end of World War Two, Onuma-sensei (center) poses in front of his archery shop

that they could find to improve upon that would not be detrimental to employees was customer service. They felt that by providing the best service in their locality they could keep their regular customers from visiting the competition and, at the same time, win new customers. The one drawback to the plan was that customer service, for the most part, is the direct responsibility of the employees. Employees were then faced with a fairly clear-cut choice: if they wanted job security, then it was their responsibility to provide the kind of quality customer service that would ensure that the business remained viable in the years to come.

The economic forecast for today's business world is not very encouraging. Even Japan, which has seen the shine wear off its economic miracle, is facing hard times. It is almost certain that as the business and economic climate changes in the coming years more and more employers will be faced with choices similar to that of our friend. Today's workers also face a choice: they can sit back and hope that the situation they enjoy now will never change, or they can take a realistic look at the business environment and accept responsibility for their own financial security by striving for excellence in everything they do.

Power and Position

In addition to his responsibilities as kyudo master, Onuma-sensei was owner of his own archery equipment shop, president and honorary chairman of the local kyudo federation and president of the national kyudo equipment association. He was also a high-ranking official in several other respected associations and organizations. Each of these positions carried a great deal of responsibility, which in every case he took very seriously. Onuma-sensei believed that people in positions of authority—company presidents, supervisors, teachers or anyone in an administrative or managerial position—are responsible not only for the success of the company or organization, but also for the well-being of the people under their care. "Companies and organizations have many rules," he said, "but there are two that should be

Members of Toshima-ku Kyudojo gather to pay their respects at the one-year anniversary of Onuma-sensei's death

honored above all else. First, always work for the good of your organization. Second, never harm anyone else in the process."

The first rule is simple enough. People in charge want their organizations to succeed; after all, their own financial and political success depends on it. Clearly the second rule poses the greater challenge. Almost anyone can make a company profitable if he is willing to show only minimal concern for the welfare of lower-ranking employees. One need only look to the success of the early industrialists who so viciously exploited the work force for personal and corporate gain. But such exploitation could not and did not go on forever. The workers eventually rose up against the bosses and fought back in a battle that took its toll on both sides. Onuma-sensei once said that a company or organization is like the human body: the head is on top, and because it sees, hears and thinks, it believes it can do anything it wants. But it must never forget that the lowly feet take it where it wants to go. Those at the top of the corporate pyramid may be responsible for the growth and success of the corporation, but they must never forget that in a real pyramid the one or two stones at the top are supported by thousands below. If the pressure from above is excessive, the base will weaken and the whole thing collapse.

It has been said that power gradually extinguishes every humane and gentle virtue from the mind. But that does not describe true power. True power is not abusive or manipulative. People who use power in that way show themselves to be interested only in politics or prestige. A truly powerful person is a leader who can get a job done without threatening or intimidating people who may have less power. And a truly powerful leader is a person who has the ability to lead anyone—even people who have as much power as he does, or more. When there are problems to be solved, the true leaders are the people who seek solutions that are beneficial to all and that hurt no one.

Onuma-sensei once recounted a story about a fellow member of an important organization. Unfortunately, this man—who had been labeled a "troublemaker"—was not living up to the expectations of the other members and the entire situation was cause for concern and debate among the membership. There was talk of voting him out—a rather drastic step in the world of Japanese organizations—but one that many thought was necessary. Onuma-sensei maintained that such a solution was charged with unforeseeable consequences and suggested that it might be better for everyone if the organization instead

Onuma-sensei leads a class, before practice, in *choshin*, a meditative breathing exercise

gave the person a position of greater responsibility. Many people thought this a foolhardy approach. But after long discussion, and Onuma-sensei's assurance that he would take full responsibility for any problems, people agreed to give it a try. As it turned out, this person seemed simply to have been in need of a little respect, because he went on to work very hard for the organization and its members and to be very successful in the position.

Our question to Onuma-sensei was how he knew that this man would live up to his responsibilities. Sensei answered that he could not be completely sure, but that he believed that the man deserved at least a chance. When asked what he would have done had the man failed, Sensei said that the reason he took full responsibility was precisely because of that possibility. Onuma-sensei felt that the man was the weakest member of the organization. And as one of the leaders Onuma-sensei considered it his own responsibility to step in and protect the man's interests. But his responsibility to the other members also meant that he had to be willing to step in and help if the person failed. That level of commitment entails a certain amount of personal and professional risk, but that, according to Onuma-sensei, is what power and position are all about.

Harmony in the Workplace

The idea of group harmony is central to Japanese culture. Harmony is known as *wa*, and *wa* in the workplace has been credited for much of the economic success enjoyed by the Japanese in recent years. We must say that *wa* is a wonderful concept that makes the work environment much more pleasant; not only for employers and employees, but for customers as well. In close to fifteen years in

Practicing for a demonstration

Japan we never once witnessed a disagreement between a supervisor and an employee, or between employees themselves. We never had to listen to a store clerk complain about working conditions, a boss or another customer. And we never had to contend with a disagreeable salesperson who was having a bad day and was taking it out on everyone around them. It is not that Japanese workers are totally happy with their work situations and have no complaints; they, like everybody else, have their share of problems in the work environment. It is merely that both employee and employer know there is a time and place for everything. Disagreement over company matters and personal grievances do not belong on the showroom floor; nor should they be aired in front of customers.

Sadly, the same cannot be said for our own country. As we write these words we have been back in the United

States for just a short time, and already we have twice been forced to wait with other customers while an employee and a supervisor worked out their differences. On countless other occasions we have had to listen to a myriad of complaints from various disgruntled salespeople in stores both large and small. Eventually we will once again become hardened to such behavior and attitudes, but until then we prefer to do as much shopping as we can by mail. Our family and friends laugh it off and tell us we have gotten too sensitive. Even though they agree that harmony in the workplace is a noble and worthwhile concept, they believe that what works in Japan would never work here.

The dictionary defines "harmony" as a state in which people are in full and perfect agreement. If that is the definition that everyone has in mind when they think of harmony then we can understand why so many people doubt that harmony will ever truly exist in the American workplace. Full and perfect agreement among people is nearly impossible; you cannot even get people to agree on how to drink their coffee, or even whether they should drink coffee. How, then, can they be expected to reach full and perfect agreement on the more complicated matters that arise at work? But the dictionary also defines harmony as cooperation between two or more people. And that is the definition that we must concern ourselves with here.

We will admit that the Japanese concept of *wa* is different from our own concept of harmony. At first glance it appears that *wa* works only because employees yield to the demands of their superiors. We once mentioned this to Onuma-sensei but he maintained that while that may sometimes be the case, it does not give a true picture of *wa*

Three women teachers at Toshima-ku Kyudojo perform a *hitotsu-mato sharei*, or shooting by three people at a single target

in the Japanese workplace. According to him, Japanese employees are more inclined to defer to the judgement of their superiors than are their Western counterparts but that *wa* is still closer in meaning to mutual cooperation between employer and employee than to simple capitulation on the part of the employee. To illustrate his point he gave the example of the special kyudo ceremony performed at advanced-level exams and demonstrations in which three or four archers shoot in concert at a single target. That type of shooting requires total cooperation among the archers, who must coordinate their individual efforts into a single, orchestrated whole to accomplish a task beneficial to all. They do this by completing their part of the ceremonial procedure with utmost perfection and grace while remaining sensitive to the actions and obligations of their fellow members. Onuma-sensei insisted that if everyone could learn to maintain that same level of cooperation in the workplace, businesses in other countries would be rewarded with some of the economic success enjoyed by the Japanese. Or, at the very least, businesses could become more pleasant places to work.

◁ 7 ▷

The Mystery of Kyudo

Every professional martial artist we know complains about needing constantly to debunk another myth or misconception about the art. It seems that the modern-day practice of martial arts is steeped in myth and magic—for the most part generated by the popularity of certain films and television programs and by the charismatic entertainers who star in them. The problem as we see it is that these films leap over the bounds of truth, presenting masters as comic book hero figures rather than the highly skilled professionals they are, and greatly exaggerating the powers to be gained from study. We are still novices in the art of kyudo so we certainly cannot speak with authority on the martial arts, but Onuma-sensei was an authority, particularly on kyudo, and although he believed that many elements of the art are beyond our understanding he would be the first to tell you that kyudo is not based on magic, although it is surrounded by mystery. This mystery is nothing more or less than the inexplicable and enigmatic. In the introduction to our first book, he wrote, "Kyudo is full of paradoxes and hidden

119

A younger Onuma-sensei in traditional ceremonial wear

truths. Each day brings a new challenge which when met yields fresh insight. Even now, after more than seventy years of practice, I continue to be fascinated by the wonderful complexity of kyudo."

Kyudo is often said to be like life itself, and not everything in life can be explained, whether by a teacher, a preacher or a scientist. Perhaps that is why life is so interesting. It is certainly why kyudo interested Onuma-sensei, and why it continues to interest us and so many others.

In this chapter we include examples of the mystery, paradox and inexplicable elements that are found in kyudo. They are presented here as they were to us—in a series of lessons and lectures, some logical and some not. As in the practice of Zen, the teachings in kyudo are often at odds with common logic. This forces the student to let the rational mind rest and bring the intuitive learning process to the fore. We hope that some of the contradictory, and seemingly unreasonable teachings presented here will help readers open themselves more to the workings of their own intuitive minds. Onuma-sensei liked to say that many things in kyudo are unreasonable, but that it is up to us to find the "reasonableness" hidden in the practice. That you do not study kyudo need not hinder your search for reasonableness in the following lessons. We study kyudo, and we still do not understand many of the teachings. Onuma-sensei insisted that the hidden truths were obvious, but that it took patience and persistence to find them. He also insisted that they were real, not imagined:

Sensei, you have told us on more than one occasion that we must find the secrets that lie hidden kyudo, but you hardly ever tell us what to look for.

The target as it appears from the shooting line

How will we know the secrets when we find them?
*They are obvious, just simple truths. Trust me, you'll
know them when you find them. But you must be the one
to search for them. All I can do is point you in the right
direction. Even if I tell you everything I have found it's of
no use to you unless you discover it again for yourself.
What value are diamonds to you if you've only heard the
story of their being found? Remember a few years ago
when I told you how the target appears to come closer
and closer until it touches the end of the arrow? For the
longest time you tried to imagine it happening, but
because it was only a story it held no real value for you.
Then one day you experienced it in the way I meant and
you immediately knew the difference between imagining*

the truth and experiencing it. It may be a long time be-fore that happens again, but when it does the truth of the experience will again be obvious.

Spirit and Technique

Once we asked Onuma-sensei, over tea, which was more important in our practice: spirit or technique. Without hesitation he said, "Spirit." But a few weeks later, during practice, he told us that our technique was poor and that we must spend more time working on it. Remembering that earlier conversation, we asked if it were possible to use the spirit to transcend poor technique. This was his answer:

I think it is possible for the spirit to transcend technique. There are stories of people accomplishing great things through the spirit alone. But I think we can only do this once. From the second time on, we invariably begin to fall back on our previous experiences, and that is how technique is born. Ultimately, we must forget about technique, but forgetting about technique is not the same as never having learned it.

When we asked if he meant that we should concentrate more on learning kyudo technique and spend less time thinking about the importance of the spirit he answered:

Technique is the stairway to the spiritual level. Students think of the study of technique as something they must endure, like some form of punishment dispensed by the teacher. They want to dispense with technique as soon as possible and move on to the more creative, spiritual aspects of study. But to learn technique you must carefully control the workings of your mind and body. And that is what students misunderstand. Controlling the mind and body does not stifle the spirit; it sets it free.

Once when we were working on patterns of movement—sitting, standing, walking—we were having trouble moving with the grace and elegance that Onuma-sensei insisted was necessary. Sensei commented that our technique lacked spirit, and that this made our movements mechanical. But when we tried to be more fluid he scolded us again, this time for being sloppy, and said, "To achieve freedom of thought and movement you must first control the mind and body through technique."

Conversely, there were periods in our study when Onuma-sensei never once spoke of technique. Even when we became so frustrated with our shooting that we would ask directly for his help with some technical point he would simply tell us to "use the spirit." This sometimes went on for weeks, and when we complained that we were being told by others that we were technically deficient in many areas he would only reply that our technique was perfect—of course, it was far from it—or that we had learned enough technique—which, of course, we hadn't. "Forget about technique," he would say. "It is holding you back. The spirit is everything. Without spirit it is a waste of time to even pick up the bow."

Illusion and Reality

The target is seductive, but the more you chase after it the more you frighten it away. You must make yourself pure in thought so that the target will come to you.

Onuma-sensei often used that analogy early in our study. It helped lessen our anxiety when we failed to hit the target after so many futile attempts. Later in our study, however, Onuma-sensei told us that it was not merely an analogy: the target actually appears to grow larger, coming closer until the tip of the arrow touches the center mark. At that point, he assured us, all you have to do is let go of the arrow and it will never fail to hit the target's center. When asked if he could teach us how to create that illusion of our own accord he insisted that it was not an illusion, but that the phenomenon was real.

To someone watching the shooting, the target appears distant and firmly attached to the target bank; that is their reality. But reality is different for the one shooting. If the person shooting is in the proper state of mind there is a real experience of the target growing larger and coming forward to touch the arrow.

But how can there be two distinct realities?

This is the result of the archer's being in a perfect state of concentration where perceptions differ from those in normal situations. When the rational mind is calmed and the intuitive mind takes over we enter into a powerful mental state that creates a new reality that is normally beyond our reach.

You know what they do to people who see a different reality; they commit them to hospitals.

[Sensei, laughing] *No, they commit the ones who get lost in this new reality and cannot get back. Creative people cross over all the time. But they have a tether that allows them to find their way back. Your mind is the tether: if it's too restrictive—if you try to rationalize and overanalyze the situation—you cannot cross over and the new reality will remain forever elusive. But if the mind is allowed to wander out of control you will become lost in the illusion.*

Believing in Yourself

Onuma-sensei believed that a human being's most powerful weapon for survival and success was the ability to believe in oneself. He went out of his way to instill confidence in his students at every turn. One of his favorite techniques was to stand nearby when a student was shooting and, just as they were about to release the arrow, whisper softly: "Never miss." In the early days of our study this constant element in our practice helped calm our nerves and later, even when we were left on our own to contend with the mental pressures of shooting, the custom of hearing his voice was so ingrained that that alone gave us the confidence to overcome self-doubt. And that

Onuma-sensei encourages a student to "Never miss"

often spelled the difference between a decent shot and a mediocre one. To this day, years after his death, both of us still hear him whisper when we shoot. Sometimes it is so real that it sends chills up our spine when we realize that he is not there beside us.

When asked about this technique Onuma-sensei said that it was hypnosis. Now, for us anyway, the term "hypnosis" immediately calls to mind images of a gimmicky stage performer embarrassing people by having them run around like a bunch of chickens. It is important to note here that Onuma-sensei abhorred that kind of manipulative control over others. He was not trying to hypnotize students; he was trying to teach them to hypnotize themselves. "Self-hypnosis simply means believing in yourself," he said, "and convincing yourself that everything is possible." It is not self-delusion. It is an expanded awareness that leaves the mind open to infinite possibilities.

Catalyst for Understanding

The following teachings were some of the most important in our study. Not only because they reveal important lessons in kyudo technique, but because they were catalysts for a deeper understanding of ourselves. These are the teachings that Onuma-sensei used to stimulate our intuitive thought processes. Most are illogical and none were fully explained. Generally speaking, we were left to fathom their meaning on our own. Some are obviously simple, at least for an experienced kyudo practitioner, but we suspect that they are not really as simple as they seem. When possible we have tried to include our personal conjectures on the possible meaning of the teachings, but in some instances we have let the teachings stand just as we received them from Onuma-sensei.

• *Keep your body perfectly straight and aligned at all times, but have a round appearance.*

This teaching came with our very first lesson with Onuma-sensei. He taught us to align our feet with the hips and shoulders, and keep them all perpendicular to the neck and spine. He also told us to keep both hands perfectly aligned and to hold the bow vertically with the arrow parallel to the floor. Both of us remember thinking the same thing: how can I keep everything straight and, at the same time, appear round? Our first hint of what he wanted came when he began to tell us to soften our bodies because we were too rigid. However, if we relaxed too much he would remind us once again to keep our bodies straight. It was not until several years later, when he began to talk about the way the spirit should not only encompass our bodies but also extend through the bow and arrow when we shoot, that we concluded that the body could be kept straight and appear round if the skeletal structure were aligned while keeping the muscles relaxed, and the spirit were sent forth in all directions.

• *You must study technique but you must never use it.*

This teaching was particularly confusing because he used it constantly in the beginning of our training when we were concentrating solely on technique. We always got the feeling that he meant it as a warning: never rely totally on technique because it is self-limiting.

• *Do not pull the string when drawing the bow.*

At first this seemed like one of the nonsensical *koans* used to test Zen monks, but experienced kyudo practitioners know that it refers to the fact that the Japanese bow,

Onuma-sensei demonstrates how to keep the body straight, yet have a round appearance

unlike its Western counterpart, is not so much pulled as spread evenly apart. Hence the admonishment never to pull the string. But Onuma-sensei also used to tell us to "let the string pull your thumb" (the Japanese use a thumb release rather than the two-finger release of Western archery) so he may have been alluding to that as well. By letting the string pull the thumb during the draw we found we could make a smooth, fluid draw while keeping the draw hand totally relaxed, allowing for a more natural release of the arrow.

- *You have no hope of hitting the target if you release the arrow yourself.*
- *Do not make the release if you wish the arrow to fly straight.*

These are twin teachings that encourage us to let the release occur naturally and spontaneously. A proper release, called *hanare* in Japanese, is one of the most perplexing aspects of kyudo practice. Here is Onuma-sensei's response to our question about the meaning of a natural release:

Sensei, you say that *hanare* is a thing of wonder, the greatest mystery in kyudo. Can you explain more about that?

It is just empty talk to discuss the mystery of hanare. *It is impossible to understand. It has been compared to snow falling from a leaf or the moment when flint strikes iron, but even these explanations have no real meaning without firsthand experience of a true, natural* hanare. *Part of the problem is that* hanare *changes as a person ages and gains experience. A young archer will have a powerful release* [described with the onomatopoeic sound

Rather than pulling the string, spread the bow and the string to left and right, applying equal pressure to each side

"kan-paan"]. *But an old master's release will be gentle* ["pe-tan"]. *It is silly for young archers to imitate the release of a master—it only results in weak shooting.* Hanare *must come from inside you. As you are, so is your release. It cannot be taught. The only thing I can tell you is to try not to make the release, then one day the release will happen naturally on its own.*

Here is another equally ambiguous teaching that Onuma-sensei used to explain the working of a spontaneous release.

• *When* hanare *is perfect your shadow will release before you do.*

This particular teaching was given to us late in our study with Onuma-sensei—in fact, only a few months before he passed away. We never had a chance to discuss it with him in any detail. It is extremely illogical and very difficult to understand. Our first thought was that it meant the same as the other teachings on *hanare*: let the release occur instinctively without thought or interference from yourself. But one day during practice we realized that our shadows were natural reflections of us. If we watched our shadows we could detach ourselves from the reality of the situation, in essence, becoming both doer and observer, teacher and student, at the same time. This proved to be an infinitely more intuitive method of studying the release on our own. Previously, when we had tried to study *hanare* without Onuma-sensei's direct assistance, we worried excessively over the precise technical elements in a natural release. We now believe that Onuma-sensei, who knew he was ill, gave us this teaching so that we could teach ourselves to better understand the mystery of *hanare* after he was gone.

After the *hanare*, or release of the arrow, Onuma-sensei's spirit continues to flow

• *Try not to think of kyudo as being difficult to learn. It is a fundamentally simple art consisting of just eight basic movements, and the shooting ceremony takes no more than a few minutes to complete. The practice of kyudo requires only that you align your body with the target, stand straight, fill yourself with spirit and shoot with a pure heart and meaningful purpose.*

• *Kyudo is the most difficult thing I have ever attempted in my life. Even now, after more than seventy years of practice, I find that I am still only a beginner.*

• *Always strive for perfection in everything you do.*

• *It is not humanly possible to be perfect.*

These last two pairs of teachings both appear contradictory. To anyone accustomed to conventional teaching methods, contradiction is tantamount to incompetency. We must admit that in the early years of our study we sometimes doubted Onuma-sensei's ability to teach. The inconsistencies in his teaching caused us no end of confusion. Luckily, this was one subject on which we did manage to elicit a fairly straightforward explanation of his intentions. When asked about these contradictions he said that he was trying to "balance our training." In a related statement he also once said, "'Natural' means 'balanced.' Too much or too little of anything—even food, water or sunshine—is unnatural." The use of contradiction was his way of shifting our thoughts and training from one extreme to the other until we found for ourselves a natural balance somewhere in between.

- *Use your entire body to move just one finger.*
- *Do not use your muscles to draw the bow; use every bone in your body instead.*
- *Spare no amount of effort to achieve effortlessness.*

These teachings were often repeated by Onuma-sensei and other kyudo teachers we knew. At first they seem to advocate the excessive use of physical effort to accomplish simple tasks, but the meaning as we understand it is totally the opposite, addressing the need to achieve a balance between spiritual and physical effort.

The target bank made of sand and earth

- *The kyudo target is difficult to hit because it does not move.*

We had never studied any other form of archery before we began to practice kyudo, and we were surprised when Onuma-sensei told us that a moving target was easier to hit. To us it seemed only logical that a moving target would be harder to hit. Onuma-sensei insisted, however, that if the mind is occupied with following the movement of the target it has less chance of deviating from its original purpose. A stationary target, on the other hand, has no lasting hold on the mind. Because the target stays in one place the mind assumes that it can freely wander from the target and safely return at will. And, as any archer or marksman will tell you, when the mind wanders it becomes extremely difficult to concentrate on hitting the target. Onuma-sensei did not directly say so but we believe he was also suggesting that this teaching could be applied to the rest of life as well. When we are actively involved with work or recreation the mind is absorbed in the activity at hand and we are content and complete, without a care in the world. But when the mind is unoccupied it begins to find small things to worry over. If we remain idle for long periods the mind begins to torment itself with bigger and bigger problems until it is consumed by its own doubt and anxiety.

- *There is no difference between hitting and missing the target.*

When we first heard this teaching we totally misunderstood it. For a long time we thought that it meant that accuracy in kyudo was unimportant. We had come to believe, through the influence of our own ideas and those of others, that kyudo was a discipline in which the results of the shooting were unimportant as long as one was "spiritually in tune" with the act of shooting. But a conversation we had with Onuma-sensei led us to a new understanding of the subject:

Sensei, if hitting the target is unimportant, why do we bother to shoot at one?
Where did you get the idea that the target is unimportant?
From you. You always say that there is no difference between hitting the target and missing it. If there is no difference, then why can't we simply shoot at an empty target bank? Without the distraction of the target we could concentrate better on the spiritual aspects of shooting.
Without the target there are no spiritual aspects. When I say there is no difference between hitting or missing the target, am I saying the target is unimportant? Can't you think a little more deeply about our purpose here? Is there anything you remember me having told you about the target?
You always say that we should see the target as an expression of our true selves. Is that what you mean?
Yes. If we use our shooting as a means of self-discovery, then—hit or miss—we learn something about ourselves every time we shoot.

• *The arrow exists in the target before the release.*
We can only assume that this teaching is similar to the one about the target's growing larger and coming closer to meet the arrow. We are both fortunate enough to have

The arrow exists in the target before the release

once had the experience of the target growing larger. This was done under the direct guidance of Onuma-sensei and we have never been able to duplicate the experience since. And even though he spent a great amount of time trying to teach us to see the arrow in the target prior to the release, neither of us has been able to do so even once. To hear Onuma-sensei tell it, the experience was real enough for him. He told us that there was a period of time in his life that lasted more than five years when he never failed to hit the target. During that time he was actually able to see the arrows—not just imagine them—in the target before the shot was made. He made a point of telling us that the arrows did not always appear in the center of the target, as one might expect if one were imagining a successful shot. Moreover, when the arrows were retrieved from the target they were always in the same position he had seen them in before he shot. He then told us that one day without warning he noticed that the target was empty. And although he would periodically experience the phenomenon throughout the rest of his life, he was never able to recreate it at will as he once could.

The Final Mystery

Onuma-sensei told us that when a great man dies, nature protests. That was never more true than on the day that he himself passed away. The events that immediately followed his death—the earthquake, the violent wind and thunderstorm and the magnificent double rainbow that arced across a sky that later was to melt into pastel shades of pink and blue—were documented in our first book. No one will ever convince us that these events were a matter of coincidence. Never before or since have we experienced such a dramatic set of events in once day. But there were

In later years

other, more personal, events of his passing that we would now like to share with our readers.

With the exception of Jackie and our son, who was too young to visit the hospital, the entire family had gathered around Onuma-sensei's bed in the moments before his death. The room was quiet except for the muted weeping of his wife and daughters and the steadily weakening tones of the system that monitored his vital signs. It was then that I realized that death was near, and I was torn with grief because I felt that I had never really had a chance to say goodbye. As Onuma-sensei drifted away, I leaned close to him and voiced a soft *kiai*—an audible manifestation of one's spirit that he had taught us—into his ear. This completely spontaneous and unexpected action on my part undoubtedly shocked his wife and other family members, but at that very instant the beat of the heart monitor responded with a quickening pace. It continued for a few moments, then gradually faded. The doctors insisted that the renewed beating of his heart was merely the result of medication that remained in his system, and that it bore no relationship to the *kiai* I had just voiced. Perhaps. But to me it was a final acknowledgment of the bond that existed between Sensei and myself. To me he was not only a great teacher, he was also a valued friend. He had said goodbye, and I could finally let him go.

At his funeral I performed a special shooting ceremony for the deceased that was part of the *Heki-ryu sekka-ha* style of kyudo—the style of traditional Japanese archery of which Onuma-sensei was headmaster. He had insisted I learn the ceremony the year before his death. At the time I thought it odd that he seemed particularly interested that I learn the entire ceremony in a relatively short period of time. Previously, when he taught me *sekka-ha*, he would take his time, often stretching out my training so that it took a couple of years or more to learn a single ceremony. He had obviously felt that his time on earth was drawing to a close.

The funeral has been largely blotted from my memory by grief but I do clearly remember preparing for it. I was given Sensei's favorite bow and arrows with which to perform the ceremony, and I remember the string breaking in

The author performs a ceremonial farewell shooting at the funeral of
Onuma Hideharu in February 1990

protest when I made a practice release on the day before the funeral. I also remember begging the bow and the string and the arrows to hold their protests until after we could honor Onuma-sensei with a final shooting.

Thankfully, they all cooperated and the shooting went off without incident. I am not sure if I performed the ceremony correctly, but I do remember thinking after releasing the string that never again would Onuma-sensei's bow produce the exquisite sounds that it had in his hands. Nor would it propel an arrow through the air and into the target as clean and true as when he was doing the shooting. The days when his spirit coursed through his arrows and bow may be gone, but the spirit of his shooting will live on in our hearts and minds, and continue to illuminate our spirit for the rest of our days.

Index